Counterfeit

—not your money but what it buys

BY ARTHUR KALLET

Co-author of 100,000,000 GUINEA PIGS

Photographs, unless otherwise credited, by the author

THE VANGUARD PRESS NEW YORK

Fourth Printing

MANUFACTURED IN THE UNITED STATES OF AMERICA BY
H. WOLFF, NEW YORK

Acknowledgment

THE author is indebted to Consumers' Research, Inc., Washington, New Jersey, for much of the data on which this book is based. Responsibility for the use made of the data, however, is solely the author's. To the many persons who have given invaluable advice and criticism, grateful acknowledgment is also due.

Prices

THE prices of products noted in the following pages are the prices paid in New York City and in New Jersey in the summer and fall of 1934, when this book was written. Many of the products vary in price geographically, from store to store, and from month to month. But since it is desired to indicate general price relationships rather than precise figures, only a single price for each product is given, as being sufficiently representative.

Contents

1. Counterfeiters

THIS is not a detective story. But it is the story of a ring of counterfeiters operating wherever money is exchanged for goods, in New York City, in Middletown, in Tompkins' Corners: a ring so bold that its plants are run openly; so powerful that the law cannot admit its existence. And the ring has so cleverly insinuated itself into the nation's life that its members are able to pose as good citizens, associating with the honest men whom they rob of billions of dollars.

The ring doesn't counterfeit money; that's a job for small-time plunderers. It counterfeits goods, and it passes off these goods in exchange for real money.

You've never heard of the ring? Why, it owns the big factories over in Millville, the department store down on Main Street, the automobile agency, and the little shops around the corner. The neighborhood drug store displays its wares. Indeed, your own house is full of counterfeit products—your furniture, your clothing, the packages of food in your pantry, the drugs in your medicine cabinet.

You Can't Play Their Game

Here is an experiment you might try if you don't mind going to jail. Copy a hundred-dollar bill. Take it to the toilet goods counter of a big department store and ask for an $11 jar of Frances Denney Herbal Throat and Neck Blend, which your ageing aunt is yearning for, having seen it advertised in the New York *Times* as a wrinkle-remover. (See page eight.) Don't offer your money until the jar is wrapped up. Then grab the package, plank down your counterfeit money, and run. Just imagine what will follow! The clerk will chase you, the manager and the store detective will chase you; soon a howling mob will join the pursuit. You will be caught before you get out of the store. You will be surrounded by swelling thousands of frantic shoppers yelling, "Thief! Robber!" Endless hordes eager for one look at the desperado will swarm in upon you. If you are fortunate, the police riot squads and the fire department will arrive in time to rescue you. You will be handcuffed and rushed to jail, photographed, fingerprinted, dragged before blinding lights in the police line-up, given the third degree to see if you had anything to do with the Astorbilt jewel theft, and finally thrown in jail for years and years by a stern and righteous judge.

But be sure to hang on to Frances Denney Herbal Throat and Neck Blend, and when you get out of jail, give it to your aunt to

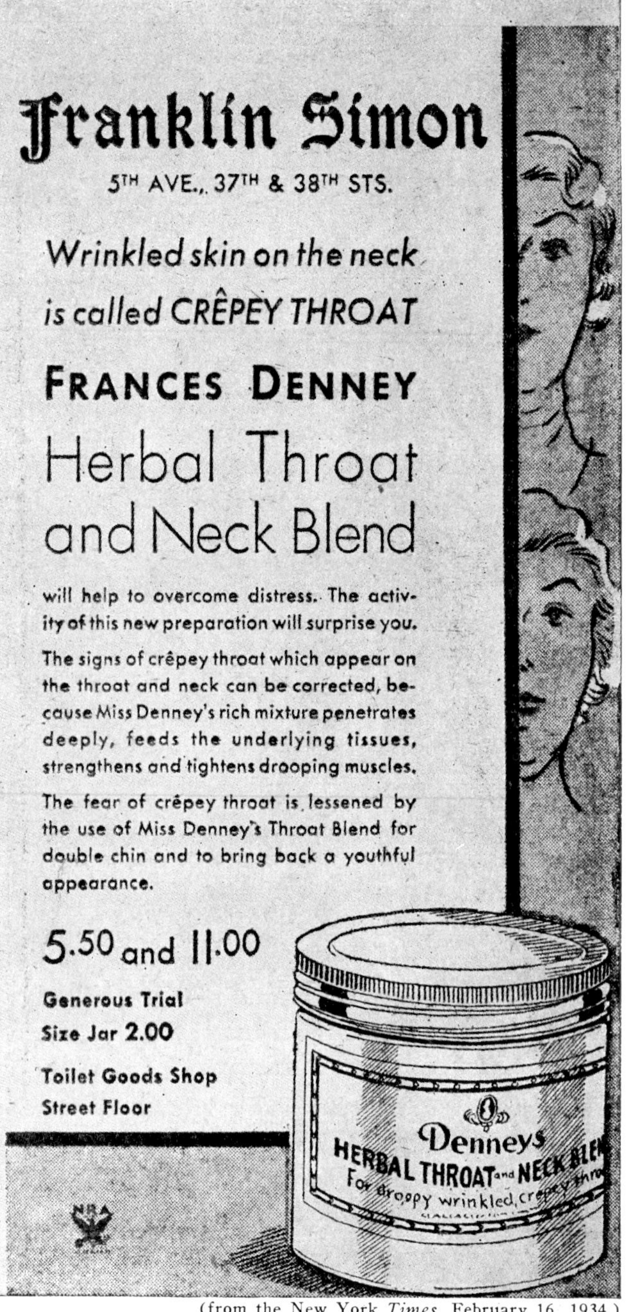
Franklin Simon
5TH AVE., 37TH & 38TH STS.
Wrinkled skin on the neck is called CRÊPEY THROAT
FRANCES DENNEY
Herbal Throat and Neck Blend
will help to overcome distress. The activity of this new preparation will surprise you.
The signs of crêpey throat which appear on the throat and neck can be corrected, because Miss Denney's rich mixture penetrates deeply, feeds the underlying tissues, strengthens and tightens drooping muscles.
The fear of crêpey throat is lessened by the use of Miss Denney's Throat Blend for double chin and to bring back a youthful appearance.
5.50 and 11.00
Generous Trial Size Jar 2.00
Toilet Goods Shop
Street Floor
Denneys
HERBAL THROAT and NECK BLEN
For droopy wrinkled, crepey thro
NRA

(from the New York *Times*, February 16, 1934.)

COUNTERFEIT!

try. In fact, try it yourself, for your ordeal will have given you wrinkles aplenty. You might also have the rest of your family try it. Soon you will discover that the number of wrinkles in your family is not fewer by even one, and that Frances Denney Herbal Throat and Neck Blend is worth no more as a wrinkle-remover than your copy of a hundred-dollar bill was as a medium of exchange. Or, to state the case differently, the jar of wrinkle cream was exactly as much a counterfeit as the money you tried to exchange for it.

But the experiment is not finished. Disguise yourself with a long black beard or a heavy veil, pick up a couple of policemen, telling them you are going to lead them to a gang of counterfeiters, dash with them into the department store, go up to the toilet goods counter, confront them with the evidence and demand the arrest of the counterfeiters. But the law has never heard of *goods*-counterfeiting. And back *you* go to jail as a maniac or at least as a disturber of the peace.

The experiment is finished. What have you learned? First, that if you try to pass counterfeit money in exchange for counterfeit goods, you go to jail even if the value of the money equals the value of the goods. Second, that if someone gives you counterfeit goods in exchange for good money, he will not go to jail; instead, he may buy a yacht or another motor car.

And there is almost nothing you can do about this kind of counterfeiting. The Better Business Bureau? Not if the counterfeiters' agent happens to be one of the large department stores which do not cut prices, for they *are* the Better Business Bureau. The Federal Trade Commission? The law gives only competitors—not victims—the privilege of protection by the Federal Trade Commission. The courts? Perhaps in one case out of a hundred, if you are willing to spend a few thousand dollars so that your great grandchildren may collect a dollar in damages.

"Honest" Counterfeiters

At this point a distinction must be made between "honest" counterfeiters and dishonest counterfeiters. On page eleven is a photograph of a blanket. On the label are the words "Part Wool." When it was purchased the store clerk was specifically asked for a blanket containing some wool—one that was not all cotton. The blanket was sent to a laboratory for analysis. Said the textile analyst's report: "100% cotton." This is clearly dishonest counterfeiting; it is represented, *in written words*, as part wool, and there is no wool in it. Let us see what an "honest" counterfeiter would do, or—better still—what an "honest" one is reported to have done. A blanket manufacturer ran a single thread of wool around the selvage of a blanket otherwise all cotton, and sold it for what it was—part wool. Blankets sold as part wool, without a definite statement of percentage of wool, usually contain as much as one or even two percent of wool; and the old wives tell about a blanket labeled "part wool" which once got on the market with ten percent of wool in it!

Many other examples of "honest" counterfeiting could be given, such as the case of the thrifty manufacturers of men's shirts. Shirts often shrink so much as to become unwearable, making the victims resolve to buy only pre-shrunk shirts thereafter. For the manufacturer, however, pre-shrinking means fewer square yards of fabric from which to make shirts, with resulting higher fabric cost. But someone discovered that fabrics could first be shrunk *and then stretched back to their original dimensions*. Of course, when this is done, the finished "pre-shrunk" shirt will shrink as much as if the fabric had never been touched, but plainly the "pre-shrunk" label is "honest."

You will say that this distinction between "honest" and dishonest counterfeiting is absurd. It is absurd. But the telling of an insignificant fraction of the truth while concealing the major truth is one of the favorite methods of respectable goods counterfeiters.

Price Counterfeiting

Another type of counterfeit will be encountered from time to time in this book. It might be called the "costly ingredient" type (with all due respect to the Pebeco Toothpaste people, who based an extended advertising campaign—and a high price for their product—on the presence of an allegedly costly ingredient; the costly ingredient being potassium chlorate, about a penny's worth in each tube of Pebeco).

Probably the greatest experts in this field are the drug and cosmetic manufacturers. They often represent their products as containing costly ingredients—perhaps the extract of a rare herb gathered at dawn by daring explorers from dangerous crags in the mountains of Tibet. Again, the costly ingredient will be Science dressed in a white coat, looking through a microscope. Sometimes the illusion of costly ingredients is created by nothing more than a very high price. Do you

"PART WOOL"
(but one little sheep would last forever)

pay five times as much for this advertised cold cream as for that unadvertised brand? Then, *ipso facto*, this brand is five times as good, and it costs five times as much to make. As a matter of fact, probably neither brand costs the manufacturer more than three or four cents a jar, and both brands are overpriced; there is also a good chance that the cheaper brand is the better. Moreover, it is possible that the two creams are identical, for sometimes one manufacturer will sell the same cream under two brand names at two different prices, to make big profits from the more credulous as a big counterfeiter and smaller profits from the wiser ones as a little counterfeiter. It's neat, and it works.

"Jewelers' Electroplate" is an example of the costly ingredient type of counterfeit. This scientific marvel was for a time the subject of a special demonstration in Gimbel Brothers Department Store in New

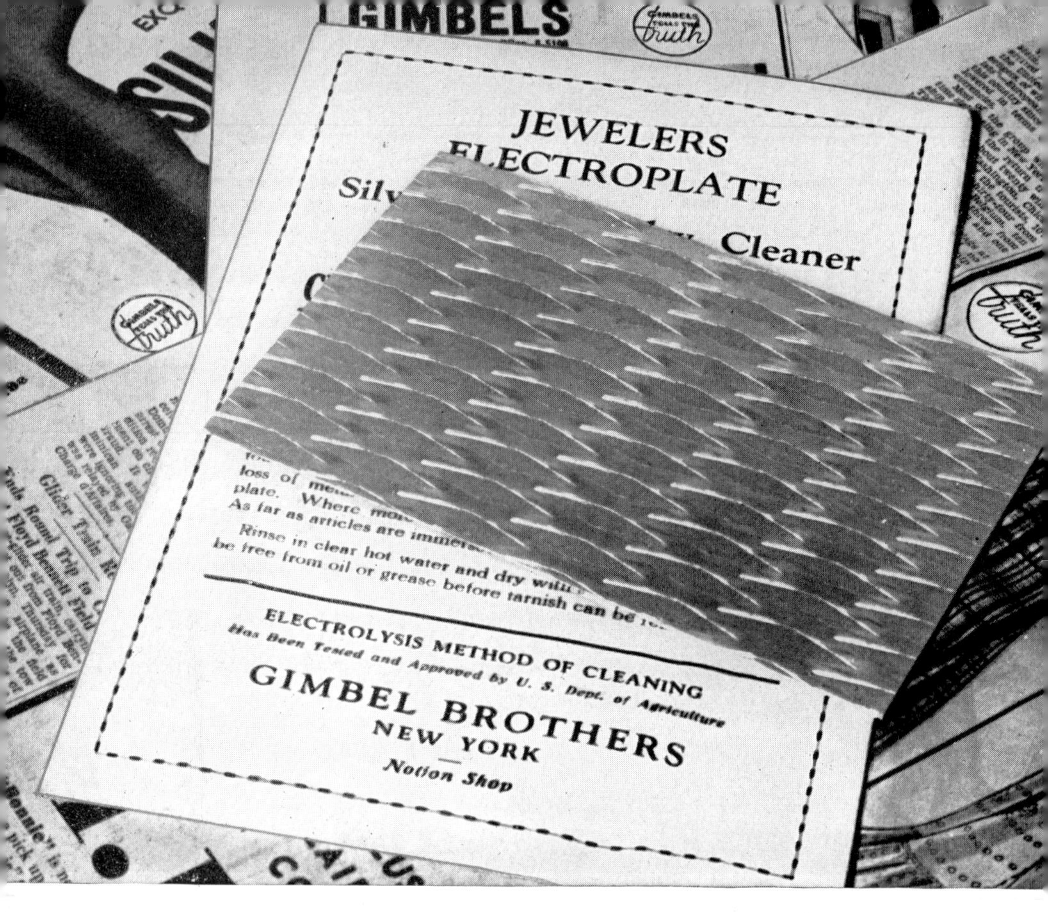

"GIMBELS TELLS THE TRUTH"
(*five metals!*)

York. The demonstrator borrowed tarnished old rings from her audience of shoppers, dipped them into a large enamelware pan containing the Electroplate and a steaming liquid (later revealed as a solution of washing soda), and returned the rings clean and bright. "This plate contains *five metals*," the demonstrator declared. "When you place your tarnished jewelry or silverware in contact with the plate, electricity passes through it, owing to the properties of these *five metals*, and the tarnish disappears. This wonderful plate is being sold today at the special price of thirty-five cents." And each of half a dozen hands held out thirty-five cents.

The "five metals" in the plate proved, on chemical analysis, to be about a half-ounce of plain ordinary aluminum—worth, at aluminum trust monopoly prices, about three-quarters of a cent. It is true that the plate will clean silverware very nicely. But so will a five-cent aluminum pot-lid or a teaball—if you place your silverware in contact with it in an enamelware pan, pour in hot water with a teaspoon each of baking soda and salt per quart, and set the pan over a flame.

There is, however, more than a method of counterfeiting goods to be learned from the "Jewelers' Electroplate." The slogan of the Gimbel Brothers Department Store is *"Gimbels Tells the Truth."*. . .

A bank teller learns to recognize counterfeit money by studying bills and coins which he knows to be counterfeit. The consumer can learn to recognize some counterfeit goods and advertising by examining the products and the advertising which he knows are counterfeit. Most of this book, therefore, is devoted to cases of goods counterfeiting. With a subject so vast, and of such limitless ramifications, it is impossible to do more than touch lightly a small number of typical cases. The reader should note that the most adept counterfeiters are not the little fellows, but the great national advertisers whose skilful handiwork appears, year after year, unchecked by time, the depression, codes of ethics, or the N.R.A.

2. Tin By The Yard

THE department store was showing this counter sign:

SALE OF SILKS—54C PER YARD

The price seemed almost too low; yet there on the counter were dozens of gorgeous fabrics that looked and felt like good silk.

"Are you *sure* this is pure silk?" the salesgirl was asked.

"Oh, yes, indeed," she replied.

"It's not weighted?"

"Weighted? What's that?"

A piece of the "pure" silk was purchased and submitted to an analyst for examination. Here is a section of the analyst's report, translated into non-technical terms:

Moisture	8%
Finishing materials which would soak off in laundering (water-soluble weighting)	14%
Metallic weighting	39%
Mineral matter	4%
Percentage of sample which was *not* silk	65%
Percentage of silk	35%

"Pure silk?" "Pure tin" or "pure lead" would have been closer to the truth about this counterfeit.

To present a complete picture, the analyst submitted additional figures making allowance for the moisture and other matter always present in fabrics. These figures showed approximately equal parts of silk and of "weighting" added to deceive the purchaser.

Unless it is clearly *labeled* "pure silk" or "pure-dye silk," the "silk" dress or the "silk" underwear or the "silk" yard goods which you buy is almost certainly a counterfeit heavily loaded with either tin or lead in the form of transparent salts. The salts impregnate the threads, making the fabric feel heavy and expensive, instead of thin and sleazy.

Studies conducted by Dr. Pauline Beery Mack and her colleagues at Pennsylvania State College showed that heavily weighted silks break and tear easily and are subject to injury from perspiration and from exposure to air and sunlight. They may deteriorate even while hanging in the closet. As for water-soluble weighting, its use can bring quick ruin to a dress accidentally splashed with water.

The silk counterfeiters are now using great quantities of lead for weighting despite the poisonous properties of this metal and the strong probability that it cannot safely be worn next to the skin.

Failure to reveal the presence of weighting in silks can be a means of unfair trade competition. The Federal Trade Commission, therefore, ruled that if a weighted silk is named as "silk," the word "weighted" must be added. In some stores this injunction is more or less faithfully observed—the more willingly because consumers generally do not know that weighted silk means counterfeit silk of decidedly inferior quality. The retailer very rarely tells the buyer the kind or the percentage of weighting. And in a great many stores, the Trade Commission's injunction has never been heard of; even the clerks do not know what weighting means; and all silk is "pure silk."

As a matter of fact, almost no pure silk is available on the market, for the Commission, moving in mysterious ways of its own, ruled that pure silk is silk containing only 10% of weighting. Practically *all* silk is counterfeit.

Silk and Tin Can
(but there's more tin in the silk than in the can)

3. Those Center Slices

When the claims of an advertiser are questioned he has a ready answer: "Oh, that's just trade puffing, just an expression of the natural pride and enthusiasm of the manufacturer for his product." (A money counterfeiter might thus justify his work because of his beautiful engraving!) Would such an excuse be acceptable if, in his exuberance, a manufacturer claimed a weight of one pound for a half-pound package? But short quality robs the consumer exactly as

The Label
("fancy—fancy—fancy")

does short weight. Consider the term *fancy*. In the trade and to government experts, "fancy," when applied to canned fruit, is a measure of quality, just as "pound" is a measure of weight. And "fancy" means *highest grade*. Compare, then, the label on the cans of Libby's "Fancy Hawaiian Sliced Pineapple" with the report of the United States Bureau of Agricultural Economics, to which cans of various brands were submitted for grading by Consumers' Research. All labels were removed, and the cans were identified and reported on by numbers. The report on Libby's pineapple, paraphrased, was: substandard because of brown color, soft and tough texture, and poor flavor.

How grade names can be used to mislead buyers is shown by the terms applied by the trade to the six grades of asparagus. The lowest of the six grades is called—"fancy"! The grade called "extra fancy" is next to the lowest; and not until we reach "colossal" do we find the highest grade.

THE CONTENTS
("substandard")

4. Skimping

THERE'S more than one way to skin a cat. And there's more than one way to make two dollars of dividends grow where only one—or none—grew before. If the profit-hunting manufacturer cannot do it simply by increasing his prices or otherwise, a "counterfeiting" method is open to him. It is known under such names as "elimination of waste," "economizing," "introduction of efficiency methods," and just plain "skimping." The consumer will prefer the last name, and in a fit of just profanity he may properly apply a more colorful term to the manufacturer who uses this method (nearly all of them do).

In the photograph opposite is part of a chair, a plain maple chair of fair line and finish; but an ordinary machine job, and high in price at $8.50. An unupholstered wooden chair such as this should last indefinitely. At the very least it should be good for 25 years. But not so this one. For the manufacturer found that he could increase his profit on the chair a cent or two by finishing the joints carelessly and by using cheap glue instead of good glue. Result: the chair, which had seemed strong and solid in the store, quickly came apart. Gain for the manufacturer, one or two cents; loss to the purchaser, about $8.

This method of making profits grow works best (1) when the consumer cannot detect the skimping at all—when he can detect only the results, and these when it is too late to do anything about it; and (2) when all or nearly all manufacturers skimp and the consumer has come to regard the result as normal.

Here are three examples of the first of these conditions: Skimping on stitching of even expensive dresses and other articles of clothing, which makes the seams pull open after a few wearings, or skimping on material allowed for seams with the same result. Gain for the manufacturer—from two or three cents to perhaps twenty-five cents. Loss to the purchaser—often many dollars. Skimping on sizes of garments, which often makes them absolutely useless after the first laundering and sometimes before. Gain for the manufacturer—not over one or two percent of the price of the garment. Loss to the purchaser—often the total price paid. Skimping on size and materials of automobile brakes, which makes them wear rapidly and work poorly under many conditions. Gain for the manufacturer—a dollar or so. Loss to the purchaser—sometimes his life. (Note: automobile manufacturers recently refused to provide a fund of a few thousand dollars needed to continue valuable research on brakes.)

And here are two examples of the second condition: skimping on quality of ingredients of all baked stuffs (including bread), of ice cream, process cheeses, soft drinks, candy and other foods which results in a generally low quality of finished product—a low quality to which the consumer has gradually become accustomed. Gain for the manufacturer—from a half-cent to half the price. Loss to the purchaser—pleasure in consumption of product, and, to a varying degree, health. . . . Skimping on quality and size of bearings of automobiles; also on quality and surface finish of metals in moving parts, paint, and general quality of materials, which shortens the life of the automobiles by more than half. Gain for the manufacturer—about $25. Loss to purchaser—several hundred dollars.

The Maker Saved Two Cents
(the buyer lost eight dollars)

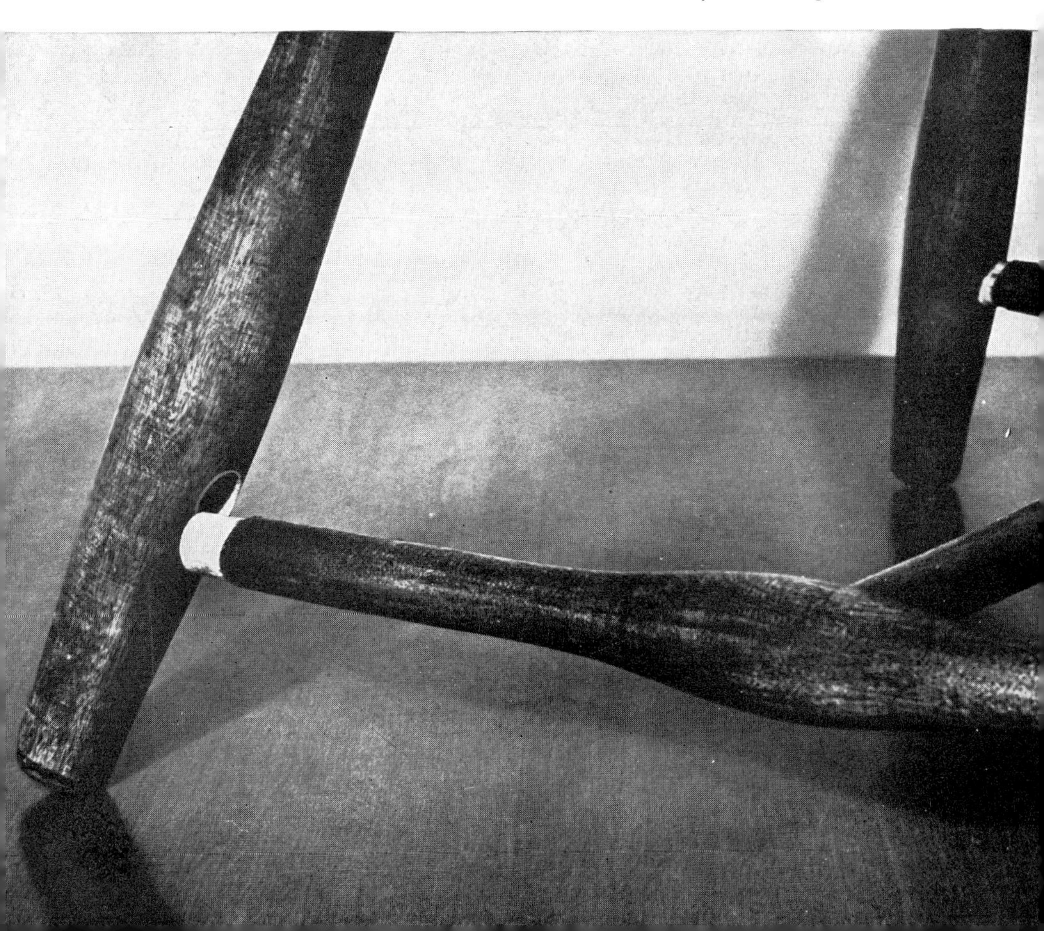

5. "It's Guaranteed!"

OH, BUT it's guaranteed," the clerk assures you. And that is supposed to resolve all your doubts and open your pocketbook. Alas, too often it does. You reason (as the manufacturer, the distributor, and the clerk expect you to reason) that the claims made—whatever the product—must be true, since otherwise they couldn't take the chance of offering you your money back, or of remedying defects.

Occasionally a guarantee is specific enough to hold water in court—if it were taken to court. But even then the guarantor takes little risk, for the purchaser is seldom willing to go to the trouble of seeking redress. He prefers to swallow his loss, vowing that next time he will shop elsewhere and know better. Probably not one out of a thousand readers of this book has escaped buying a dress or a shirt or linens guaranteed not to fade or shrink, but which actually did fade or shrink. And probably not two out of a thousand have attempted to seek fulfillment of the guarantee.

Just what does the average guarantee mean, for example, the guarantee on the label of the undershirt shown in the photograph? Absolutely nothing.

Ironized Yeast is "guaranteed." Says an advertisement: "Results Guaranteed. No matter how skinny and weak you may be, this marvelous new Ironized Yeast should build you up in a few short weeks as it has thousands. If not delighted with the results of the very first package, money back instantly." In a report on Ironized Yeast which carries the conclusion that this is just one more worthless nostrum, the Bureau of Investigation of the American Medical Association thus analyzes the guarantee:

> "It takes careful reading of this alleged 'guarantee' to show what it means. It will be noted that the company does not state that Ironized Yeast *will* 'build you up in a few short weeks' but that it *should!* Furthermore, while the careless reader might get the impression that he could take Ironized Yeast for the three months that are recommended (at a cost of $21.60) and at the end of that time, if he is not satisfied, could get his 'money back instantly,' this is not what the 'guarantee' says. What it does say is that he must be dissatisfied with the results of the 'very first package' (one dollar's worth). As one could hardly expect a transformation from emaciation to plumpness in the four days that a package lasts, the value of the 'guarantee' is obvious."

Or consider this typical guarantee for a mechanical-electrical appliance:

"WE HEREBY GUARANTEE this washer [Whirldry] for household use for a period of one year from date of purchase against all defects in material or workmanship; except ordinary wear, chipping of the porcelain enamel on the tank, accidents or misuse.

"WE AGREE to replace without charge for the above period any defective parts delivered to us at our factory prepaid." (Why the purchaser should pay express charges if materials or workmanship are faulty is not explained.)

"This Guarantee is not binding on us unless this washer is used in accordance with our printed instructions. . . ."

But who is to decide whether the defect is in materials or workmanship, or is due to ordinary wear or misuse? The manufacturer, of course.

GUARANTEED TO BE UNDERWEAR?

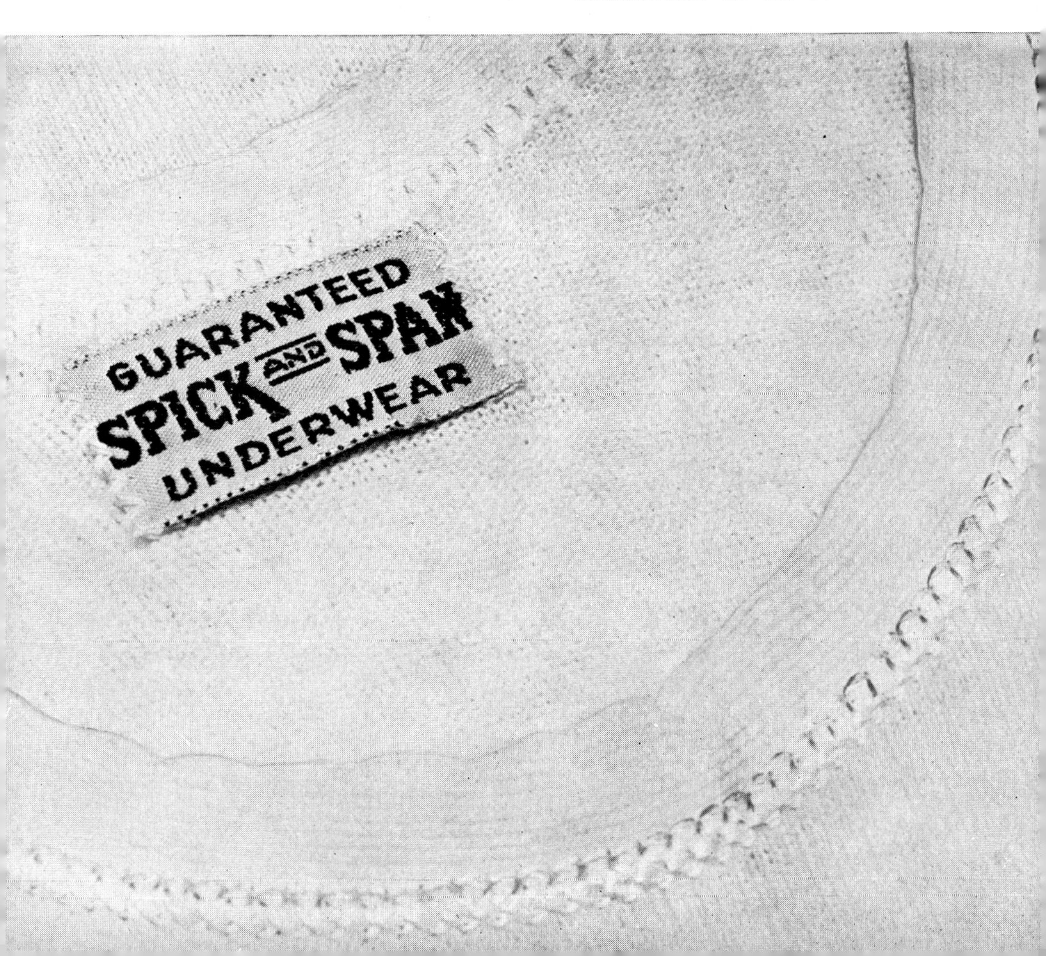

How do you find out whether the manufacturer is responsible for a defect? Hire a mechanic to remove the part, crate or pack it and ship it to the factory at your own expense. If the manufacturer kindly decides to replace it, the new part will be shipped to you (perhaps charges collect) and you can then hire the mechanic to put it back.

Or consider the typical automobile guarantee. Again, the manufacturer or the sales agency decides whether the purchaser or the material is at fault. If it is decided that you are not responsible, the manufacturer supplies the necessary replacement parts, at trivial cost to him—but *you* pay for the labor, and as often as not you pay with a vengeance. As a Ford salesman once admitted—after a sale, and when a repair was demanded—"the guarantee doesn't mean a damned thing."

Merchants, aided by obliging women's clubs, have been carrying on a campaign against the return of merchandise. While some returns are unquestionably not justified, the fact remains that a large percentage of all goods sold is misrepresented and ought to be returned, particularly where there is a guarantee, expressed or implied. You will do well to check up carefully on performance of things you buy in relation to claims and to guarantees, and to return the goods and demand fulfillment of guarantees if performance fails. If possible, refuse to buy unless the seller makes the guarantee a good one. Insist that it be unconditional, applying to all degrees of nonperformance and to all defects, with you the sole judge of nonperformance or defect. If you accomplish nothing more, you will at least gain a better insight into the manufacturer's or merchant's attitude toward his product.

6. Soap Is Soap

ONCE upon a time, in the unromantic past, soap was something to wash yourself with. Today, soap makes you a movie star, or at least as beautiful as one, and it brings back lost loves, lost youth, and lost jobs. If you suppose that scientists have actually discovered one single little ingredient which would give soap a ten-thousandth part of the marvelous properties claimed for it monthly, weekly, and daily, in acres of pages in women's magazines and endless blurbs over the radio, you do not understand the ways of the counterfeiters. The claims have nothing to do with the properties of soap, which is still just something to wash yourself with. The superabundance of advertising merely reflects the large profits to be made from the manufacture and sale of soap and the intense competition for this lucrative business. And the claims reflect only the natural desire of women to be beautiful. Advertisers boast that they find out what people want and

35¢ FOR A GOOD NAME
(6¢ for a good soap)

give it to them. Seldom is this correct. Normally their function is to find out what people want, and then claim it for their products.

What can soap honestly do? Curiously enough, we find the answer for any soap in a Camay advertisment: "Camay does one thing . . . Camay cleanses the skin!" And that is all Camay or any other toilet soap can do. This particular advertisement appeared in the *Journal of the American Medical Association*. In the *Ladies' Home Journal*, however, we read that "Even the girl with plain features can be lovely to look at. If her complexion has the peach-bloom quality—the smooth, clear texture that Camay, the Soap of Beautiful Women, gives the feminine skin, she'll be admired wherever she goes."

Forty different brands of toilet soap ranging in price from five cents to 50 cents per cake were tested by Consumers' Research. Of all of these none had a finer name than Yardley's, but the tests placed Yardley's fifth from the bottom of the list. Let us compare two soaps, Yardley's at 35 cents per cake and Sweetheart Soap at six cents per cake, as a chemist would compare them on the basis of tests made by Consumers' Research:

	PERCENT	
	YARDLEY	SWEETHEART
Moisture	8.4	7.8
(The higher this figure is, the more water you are buying at soap prices)		
Matter insoluble in alcohol	.6	.4
(Irritating to some skins. This figure should be as low as possible)		
Free alkali	0.0	0.0
(Irritating—should be as low as possible)		
Free acidity	.4	0.0
(May be irritating to some skins, should be as low as possible)		
Matter insoluble in water	.3	.1
(Filler—does not belong in toilet soap)		
Sodium chloride	.3	.3
(The more carefully a soap is manufactured, the less sodium chloride will remain in it)		

The comparison, as you see, shows Sweetheart soap (6¢) superior to Yardley's soap (35¢) on four points, equal to it on two, and inferior on none. Perhaps you want the scent of lavender? The oil of lavender used in soap and cosmetics is one of the least expensive of fragrances, and for 35 cents you can buy enough of the natural lavender to scent your bathroom, your bedroom, and, if you must, your whole house for a long time.

Let us appraise a few of the widely advertised soaps in the light of the Consumers' Research tests:

Woodbury's (The skin you love to touch): A soap of average quality, poorer than many cheaper soaps. Claims unwarranted.

Camay (The soap of beautiful women): Average quality. Claims unwarranted.

Lux (You can have the kind of skin the screen stars have): Average quality. Claims unwarranted.

Palmolive (That schoolgirl complexion): A good soap. Claims unwarranted.

Cashmere Bouquet (The complexion benefits that only a soap so fine can give): Good soap but expensive. Claims unwarranted.

Conti Castile (Labeled as meeting the U. S. Pharmacopoeia standards): Tests showed it did not comply with all Pharmacopoeia requirements. Castile soaps in general are unreliable and frequently poorer than ordinary toilet soaps.

Lifebuoy (B.O.): Contains rosin which is undesirable in a toilet soap. No more efficacious than any other soap in destroying odors.

Pears' Unscented Transparent Soap (The soothing help only Pears' can give your complexion): Low quality. Contains rosin. Claims unwarranted.

To sum it all up, a good toilet soap is one containing a minimum of unnecessary and irritating ingredients or residues. A poor soap is potentially irritating, at least to sensitive skins. And the enticing claims of the soap advertisers are counterfeit.

7. The Seven Deadly Stains

WHERE the soap counterfeiters leave off, the toothpaste counterfeiters begin. No claim is left untried in the long gamut from sex to science. Colgate's toothpaste will positively get you a husband (formerly repelled by the seven stains on your teeth). Kolynos will bring you love, popularity, whatever you wish, by making your teeth three shades whiter in three days. You can dress more attractively with the money you save by using Listerine toothpaste (on the theory that a *small* tube of Listerine at 25 cents is more economical than a *large* tube of some other toothpaste at 40 cents!). "What a FOOL she is!" exclaims the Ipana advertisement. By using Ipana, she will end her foolishness, her "pink toothbrush," and the terrible danger of gingivitis and Vincent's disease! With Pepsodent, we get down to real science. Pepsodent removes the FILM "laden with millions of tiny germs." And Squibb's scientific toothpaste "combats the germ acids that cause tooth-decay" (at least it did before the American Dental Association withdrew its seal of approval from Squibb toothpaste because of the claims made for it).

This is the status of tooth cleansers according to such authorities as the American Dental Association: no toothpaste safe for daily use on the teeth will prevent or cure pyorrhea or other diseases of the gums; no safe toothpaste will whiten teeth; nor effectively combat excessive mouth acidity; nor prevent decay; in fact, no toothpaste can be anything more than a slight aid to the mechanical cleansing of the teeth. And precipitated chalk or a mixture of precipitated chalk with a little bicarbonate of soda, used as a toothpowder, will serve just as well. A pound of precipitated chalk—about a year's supply for a small family—can be purchased in almost any drug store for 35 or 40 cents.

Evidence continues to accumulate that while toothbrushing is advisable, it is only a minor factor in the prevention of tooth decay. Probably diet is of far greater importance. But no one has yet succeeded in proving that any particular diet will certainly prevent decay, or that any particular foodstuffs have supreme merit in inhibiting decay. A sufficient intake of vitamins C and D appears to be necessary, but you can get enough vitamin C, even if you never look at an orange or a lemon, the highly "scientific" propaganda of the citrus growers to the contrary notwithstanding, and it is not necessary to eat special irradiated proprietary foods for vitamin D. Cereals appear to have a harmful effect on the teeth, and probably

$2.75 WORTH OF TOOTHPASTE = 7¢ WORTH OF CHALK
(but the chalk won't make you popular)

should not be given to growing children in large amounts. What has been already established, however, in relation to diet and teeth makes one thing fairly certain: millions of American children badly fed or going hungry because their fathers are earning N.R.A. minimum wages or less, or are on relief, will have bad teeth for the rest of their lives.

8. The Gargle Gang

High honors for expert counterfeiting must go to the makers of mouth washes. The few mouth washes in the picture are representative of hundreds. What is claimed for them?

"The amazing results of Pepsodent Antiseptic in fighting sore throat colds prove its effectiveness in checking Bad Breath (Halitosis).* Some of the 50 different uses for this modern antiseptic—Sore Throat Colds—Head Colds—Smoker's Throat—Bad Breath—Mouth Irritations—Irritations of the Gums—After Extractions—After Shaving—Cuts and Abrasions—Chapped Hands—Dandruff—Skin Irritations—Checks Under-arm Perspiration Odor—'Athlete's Foot'—Tired, Aching Feet."

"Use in your own home, at the first sign of cold or sore throat, the modern antiseptic [Hexylresorcinol S. T. 37] that great hospitals are using. . . . The minute you feel a cold or sore throat coming on, gargle with it."

"More than 20 different children's diseases are said to originate in the mouth. This is the reason so many physicians and dentists advise a daily *oral purge* in the case of growing children. Not a mere antiseptic gargle—but a mouth and throat *purging* gargle that flushes out germ-breeding mucus. Lavoris . . . *purges* the mouth and throat, thus the dangerous germs *embedded* in the mucous coating are actually and effectively removed."

* How does this prove it?—Which tells you all you need to know about the advertisers' conception of scientific proof.

"Actual tests have shown that Listerine users got fewer colds than non-users. Moreover, when they did contract colds, the colds were mild and of short duration. The moment Listerine enters the oral cavity, it begins to kill millions of germs—including those associated with colds and sore throat. Within 5 minutes the number of bacteria have been reduced as much as 99%."

Other claims of the same type are made for Astringosol, Glyco Thymoline, Dr. Lyon's Mouth Wash, Cal-So-Dent, Zonite, and a host of other high-priced mouth washes. Are they necessary to good health, or even useful?

The following, quoted from the Consumers' Research *Handbook of Buying*, provides an answer:

"No proprietary mouth wash is needed, useful or effective in the ways usually claimed. The healthy mouth does not need a remedy and certainly not a mouth wash—persistent use in the normal mouth may indeed be harmful; the unhealthy mouth will require more definite and specialized treatment than use of a proprietary mouth wash. Antiseptics capable of actually sterilizing the tissues of the mouth will destroy them, and if sterilization were possible it could last but a few minutes at best."

9. Beans

CAMPBELL'S Pork and Beans finds its way into these pages only because its price to the ultimate consumer is five cents. (We are not concerned here with the quality of the can's contents.) The five cents covers the cost of the pork and beans, labor, canning and processing, the can, the label, plant and machinery, superintendence,

5¢
(something to remember)

general overhead and profits, and distribution costs, including transportation and retailers' profit. The manufacturer could pay a decent price to the farmer and a living wage to the worker and still keep the price to the consumer under seven cents.

You may be wondering how Campbell's beans enter into this story of goods counterfeiting. This is the reason: many products that cost less than Campbell's beans for ingredients, labor, and other production costs sell for from ten to thirty times as much as the can of beans. "High distribution costs" is advanced as an explanation of these high prices. High *counterfeiting* costs would be a better explanation: the costs involved in carrying the tremendous merchandising and advertising burden of creating and maintaining for a product of little or no intrinsic merit the illusion of value and necessity.

It costs little to sell a can of beans. But take a product that can serve no useful function, and try to create in millions of minds the illusion that the product is indispensable to health or happiness. Hire merchandising and advertising geniuses at huge salaries. Proclaim the fancied virtues of the product in magazine and newspaper advertisements, on car cards and billboards, and over the radio. Offer samples, souvenirs, and prizes. Buy testimonials from "scientists" and Social Registerites. Of course the selling cost is high! But if the counterfeiters are clever enough, if the illusion of vital necessity is created in enough minds, the profits also are high.

The plaint of high distribution costs is as often applied to genuinely useful products, such as automobiles, refrigerators, radios, and washing machines. Here, too, counterfeiting cost is often heavy: the cost of creating the conviction that only the Jones brand or the Smith brand and no other brand whatsoever will make the prospective purchaser happy.*

The can of beans will help you to understand that high prices are not the result of *necessary* high distribution costs. When business writers talk mysteriously about high distribution costs, remember the can of beans.

---

* In such cases, however, the counterfeiting cost is often trivial in comparison with tremendous production and distribution wastes of other types inherent in that individualistic, uncoordinated, competitive production and distribution which is a boasted characteristic of capitalist economy.

10. Charge All The Traffic Will Bear!

CHARGE all the traffic will bear! This is the absolute injunction of a counterfeit economic system. Mr. Manufacturer, charge for your products not costs plus a fair margin of profit, not a price low enough to give the product the widest possible distribution, but charge the price that will bring you the largest profit.

The photograph on the opposite page illustrates the working of "Charge all the traffic will bear." Clorox and Zonite are essentially similar solutions in which chlorine is the active ingredient. Clorox is sold through grocery stores primarily for use in home laundering. Most of the housewives who do their own laundry belong in one of two income groups: the first, and larger, group, those whose income is so low that they frequently cannot buy even soap. Obviously, this is not a good market for Clorox. The second, those whose income is higher but still too low to permit their use of commercial laundries, provides the natural market for such a product as Clorox. What is the maximum amount that large numbers of these women will pay for a laundry aid? The figure set was fifteen cents for a 16-ounce bottle.* Presumably, had the price been set higher, there would have been more profit per bottle, but the smaller volume of sales would have cut the total profits; if the figure had been set lower, there would have been more sales, but not enough more to make up for the smaller profit.

Put the same ingredients, in a much weaker solution, in a Zonite bottle, and the story is different. Here is no lowly laundry aid, but a wonderful germ-destroying mouth wash; a "modern personal antiseptic" to ward off disease, and for "feminine hygiene." Who are the potential buyers of this product? Some wives of millionaires and sub-millionaires. They do not count, however, for there aren't enough of them. The people who are too poor to buy Clorox certainly do not exist as Zonite prospects. All the rest count, including those with plenty of money and those with so little money that the purchase of a "modern personal antiseptic" will mean going without meat at the end of the week. To bring in the largest profit from this potential market, Zonite is now sold for 81 cents for a 14-ounce bottle. Why was a high price possible? Because counterfeit advertising was counted upon to persuade consumers that here was a product out of the

* In connection with this and other prices see note on the Acknowledgment page.

ordinary—one absolutely necessary to health. Apparently the decision was justified by the results, although Zonite is not at all necessary to health, and is unsuitable and even unsafe for many of its advertised uses. A few years ago the Zonite Company was paying in dividends over 100 per cent on the par value of its shares.

You may have noticed that the Zonite bottle at 81 cents contains two ounces less than the Clorox bottle at 15 cents. But this difference in cost and quantity is trivial in comparison with other differences between Zonite and Clorox. Clorox is five times as strong as Zonite—that is, it can be diluted with five times as much water to give the same strength solution. Therefore one 16-ounce bottle of Clorox is equal to five and one-half 14-ounce bottles of Zonite. A proper comparison of prices shows that 15 cents worth of Clorox is equal to $4.45 worth of Zonite; or, less than 3 cents worth of Clorox is equivalent to an 81-cent bottle of Zonite. Charge all the traffic will bear!

THE TRAFFIC BEARS

(the relative "bearing power" of a laundry aid and a "modern antiseptic")

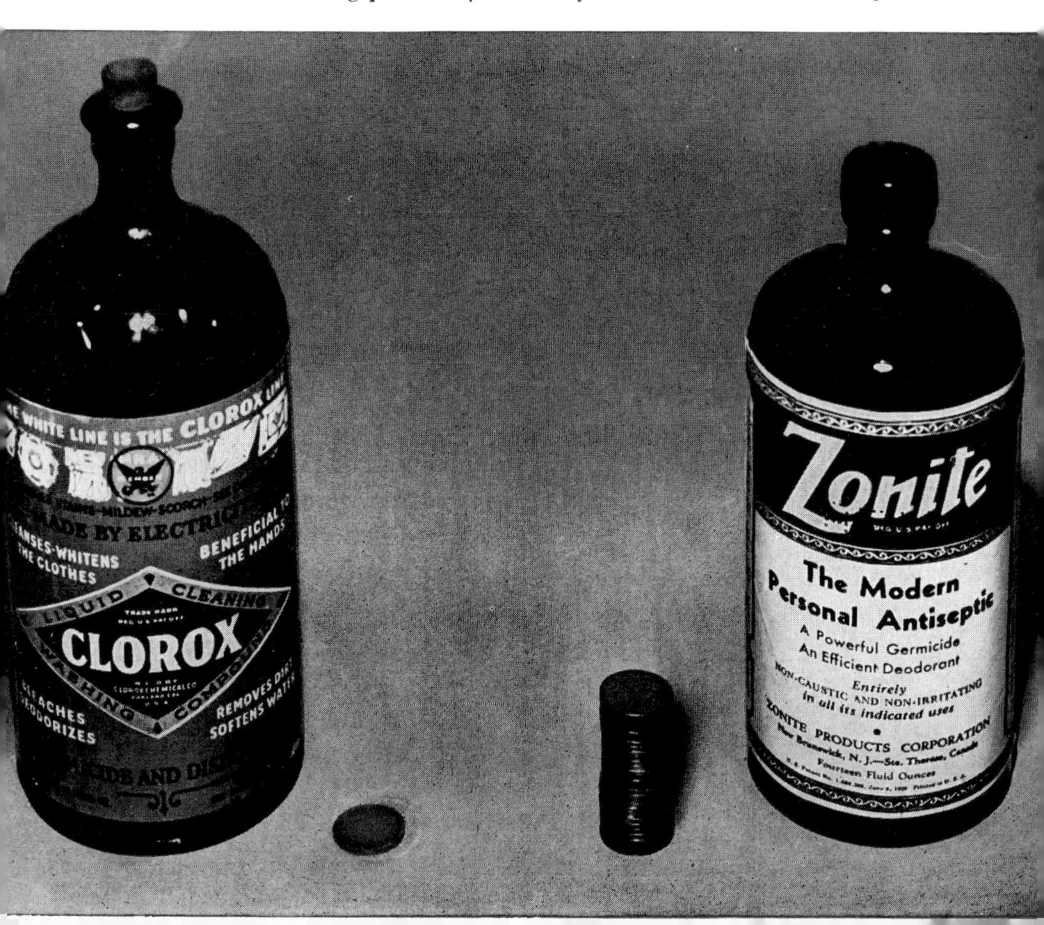

11. Not So Crazy

A VOICE as doleful as an undertaker's, mournful music, heartrending songs. You are listening, friends of the radio audience, to the Crazy Water Crystals program. But why the gloom? Here, if anywhere, all should be joy and merrymaking. For it is not merely the Crazy Water company broadcasting; it is one of the shining examples of the dizzy heights to which rugged individualists can climb under the profit system. "Charge all that the traffic will bear," the system commands. And how this company has been able to make the traffic bear and bear! For the equivalent of a few cents' worth of Glauber's salt—a plain, ordinary old-fashioned cathartic of not the best medical repute, packed in a quite undistinguished carton with an ordinary jacket of cellophane—multitudes of consumers have been persuaded to pay $1.50.

Another term for "making the traffic bear" is counterfeiting. The directing geniuses of the Crazy Water company are superb counterfeiters. This cellophane-wrapped carton does not contain Glauber's salt; those who listen to the Crazy Crystals broadcasts are led to believe that it contains marvelous crystals, endowed with metaphysical properties, which bring the benefits of a great health resort into your home. Have you bad complexion, bad breath, acid stomach, biliousness, rheumatism, arthritis, neuritis, aches and pains, kidney ailments, colds? Then you are exactly the person who needs these marvelous crystals—crystals which are not manufactured, but are actually obtained by natural evaporation from famous health springs. In them are concentrated all the wonderful ingredients of the springs. (It is true that there is a small percentage of other ingredients, one of these a rare chemical known as sodium chloride—some call it table salt. Another is sodium carbonate—called washing soda by housewives.) The crystals may, in fact, be obtained by evaporation, since this is a cheap way of getting Glauber's salt, but there is not the faintest shred of evidence that Glauber's salt obtained by evaporation from a "health spring" differs in its physiological action by so much as the weight of an electron from ordinary Glauber's salt from other sources. As to the other ingredients of the crystals, a better name for them would be impurities. The company's claim that these ingredients have effects which could not be duplicated if the same ingredients were put together by a chemist is just more metaphysics. And advertisers' metaphysics is better described as *bunk*.

None of Crazy Crystals' advertising makes mention of certain *other* important ingredients which were discovered by the chemists of the Federal Food and Drug Administration. Sixteen times, between 1913 and 1928, shipments of Crazy Water Crystals were seized by Federal inspectors for false and fraudulent curative claims. In the government *Notices of Judgment* explaining 14 of the 16 seizures, these certain other ingredients were described by the scientifically loose but adequate term of "filth."

WHAT $1.50 BUYS

(14 ounces of crazy crystals in the drug store, or 25 pounds of Glauber's salt in a chemical supply house)

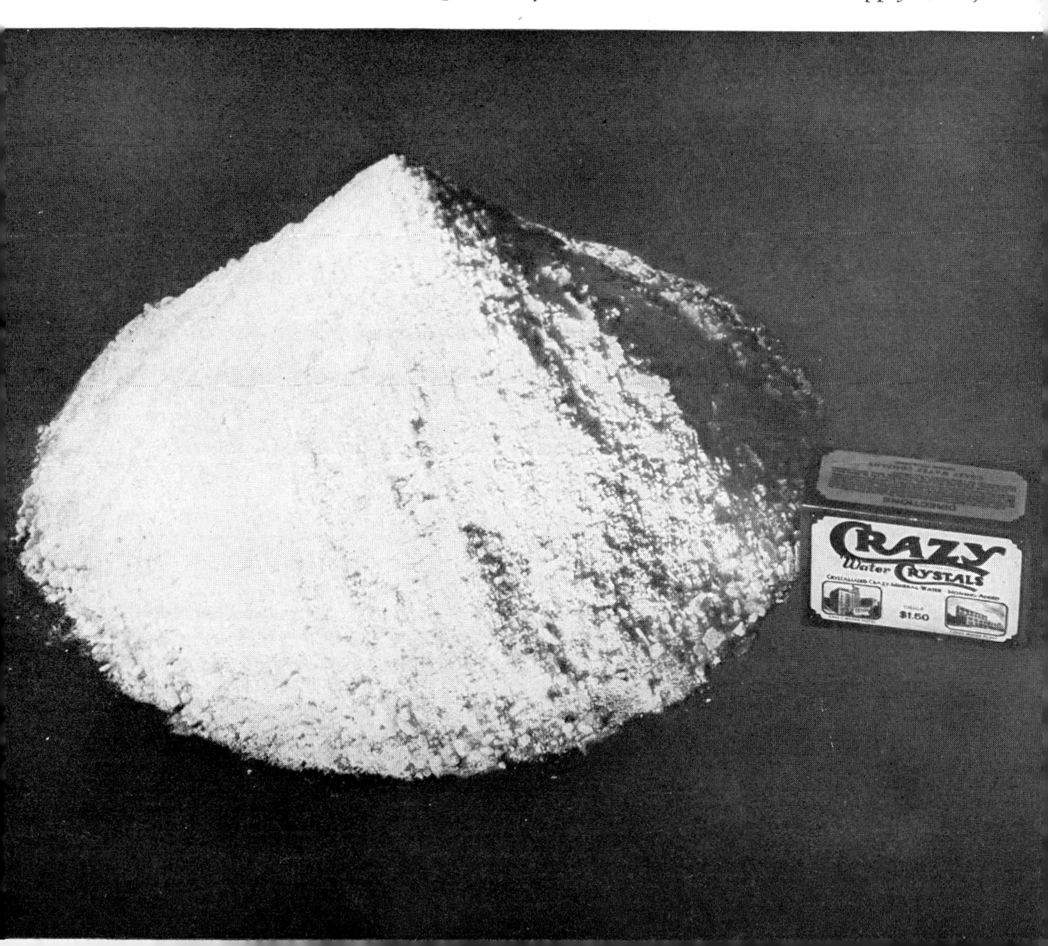

12. A Few That Made Good

CHARGE all the traffic will bear! It is illuminating to examine several products which have gone out into the traffic and made good.

In the photographs, there are piles of coins in front of each product. The left-hand pile represents the cost of the product to the consumer. The next pile represents an estimate of the cost of the ingredients of the product at wholesale. The third pile, where there is one, represents a very rough estimate of the true worth of the product to the consumer. In some cases, the true worth should be represented by a minus quantity, since the product is hazardous to health or otherwise potentially far more costly than its price. Since it is impossible to evaluate such costs, the "worth" pile is simply omitted.

Crazy Water Crystals: This product has already been discussed, but as a masterpiece of price counterfeiting it demanded inclusion in the photograph. The worth to the consumer is considered minus because the continual consumption of salts can be seriously injurious.

Forhan's toothpaste: This paste was made a best seller by an "educational" advertising campaign informing the world that 4 out of 5 are afflicted with pyorrhea, and that Forhan's prevents pyorrhea. Both claims are false. A cent's worth of precipitated chalk is an excellent substitute for a tube of Forhan's; hence the penny valuation.

Carbona: The "fabricating" cost for toothpaste is so small as to be negligible, but for Carbona it doesn't exist. Carbona is just one chemical, carbon tetrachloride, unaltered, worth about five cents per pound in large quantities. A selling price of forty-eight cents for a nine-ounce bottle nets a very nice profit. Carbon tetrachloride is

indeed a fairly satisfactory cleaner. Why then the minus valuation? The label says "For Safety, Carbona Cleansing Fluid." It is *not* safe. Carbon tetrachloride is poisonous when inhaled, and, in the opinion of some authorities, when in contact with the skin. Carbon tetrachloride vapor, in heavy concentration, has caused many deaths.

Ambrosia: Facial astringents such as Ambrosia are of extremely doubtful value. Probably they can do no more than ordinary witch-hazel. Ambrosia goes on the minus list because it contains carbolic acid, which can cause serious injury to some skins.

Larvex: The manufacturer's cost of the contents of a large bottle of Larvex is so small that a single penny grossly exaggerates it. It costs you 79 cents. That is, the immediate cost is 79 cents. But no spray adequately protects woolens against moths, and if you depend upon Larvex the loss may be many dollars. Hence the minus value.

A. B. Dick Mimeograph Ink: This product is included by way of balm to the ultimate consumer, if it is balm to him to know that big corporations, too, sometimes are taken in by price-counterfeiters. The Dick company practically monopolizes the mimeograph machine market, and it persuades the users of its machines to buy its ink at $2.50 per pound, sometimes refusing to service the machines if other inks are used. The U. S. government standard mimeograph ink costs about 12 cents per pound for ingredients and a few cents for compounding. And the Dick ink, according to experts, costs no more than this. The "worth" pile of coins represents the price at which a government monopoly might sell the ink.

13. Milk Money

WHEN the goods counterfeiters turn out ten-dollar cosmetics, one can be amused; but when the counterfeiters are milk distributors there is no more humor in their operations than there is in an epidemic of infantile paralysis. Here is a product which children must have; which should be produced, pasteurized, and distributed under perfect sanitary conditions and sold at the lowest possible price—a price which would not permit huge salaries to officers and executives (a customary means of disguising large profits), and expensive advertising campaigns. In other words, here is an industry which cries to heaven for public operation.

Instead, milk distribution is carried on like any other private enterprise, which means that the big distributors who control prices pay as little as possible to farmers and charge consumers as much as possible. The result is that, despite many exceptions, this easily contaminated product is often produced under filthy conditions, and with the prices paid him the farmer cannot improve these conditions even if he wants to. If the milk is not pasteurized it is usually—except for the product of some (not all) "certified" plants—not fit for human consumption. Furthermore, because of the contamination of the raw milk, and because of improper pasteurizing and the unsanitary condition of the pasteurizing plant, much pasteurized milk is unsafe. Finally, the prices are so high that millions of children either go without milk or drink far too little.

The counterfeit consists primarily in the claim that this milk is generally safe and wholesome. It is not. But the counterfeiting does not end there. In those areas where milk is sold as Grade A and Grade B, some companies lead the public to believe that the Grade A bottles contain better and purer milk than the Grade B bottles, and then put milk from the same vats into bottles of both grades. The difference in price between the grades is usually three cents per quart. For each quart of Grade A milk purchased daily from these companies, parents who cut their own limited food allowance to provide this milk for their children are permitted to contribute about ten dollars per year (three cents per day) to the companies' profits. Even where there is an actual difference between the grades the extra three cents is largely extra profit. It is for this reason that large distributors who sell both Grade A and Grade B carry on big advertising campaigns for their Grade A milk. Nor is it without effect that they put an unsanitary cap on Grade B bottles and often deliver the bottles with a plentiful layer of dirt. The hood that is placed over the top of Grade A bottles could be put on Grade B bottles as well with no increase in Grade B price and with insignificant effect on profits.

It will do no good to make milk a public utility, as many have proposed. The milk companies would control the utility commissions just as they now control milk commissions. There will be counterfeiting in the milk industry until milk and profits are separated.

THREE CENTS FOR A CAP
(and $10 more for dividends)

14. It Didn't Hurt The Rats!

If you are an average consumer, you do not find it hard to believe that your pocket is courteously picked almost every time you exchange your money for the products of industry. But Mr. Average Consumer is often shocked to discover that manufacturers and those who help them sell their products are willing to rob him of his health and even of his life if they can make money by doing so. This is so natural a part of our economic system that our laws and their enforcement are designed to protect those who injure and kill in the regular course of legitimate business as surely as the laws protect those who merely cheat us.

Here are two examples out of the past of gross disregard for the consumer's welfare:

1. Around the time of the passage of the first pure food and drug legislation, many infants were killed by a "baby-soother" containing morphine. Several years later the manufacturer was fined $25 for *misbranding* this deadly poison. He wasn't even required to stop making and selling it!

2. Two men met horrible deaths, a few years ago, from drinking a medicinal water into which the manufacturer, an ex-stock-swindler, had put radium. He was neither imprisoned nor fined. His career as a killer was stopped by the Federal Trade Commission only because he was competing unfairly with other business men.

Countless examples could be given of similar disregard for the consumer's welfare in products now on the market. Kellogg's All-Bran is chosen as an example because it is nationally advertised and sold, because the consumer is not generally aware of the hazard of this product, and because the testimony of authorities leaves little doubt that in the aggregate and considering the great number of persons who take bran constantly, it is far more dangerous than the two products cited above.

The probable extent of this damage being done by the millions of cartons of All-Bran sold to consumers can be judged from the following statement by Dr. W. Gerry Morgan, made in the course of a radio broadcast sponsored by the United States Public Health Service:

> "Whereas approximately a third of those eating bran are able to take it over an indefinite length of time without apparent harmful results, and even with temporary relief from a constipated condition, yet by far the

BRAN IS NOT SANDPAPER, BUT. . . .

larger proportion of bran eaters develop a deep seated irritation in one part or another of the intestinal tract. It is the opinion of excellent authorities that this irritation is often the fundamental condition leading to ulceration by producing localized areas of congestion and superficial loss of the mucous membrane, thus creating a suitable field upon which subsequent disease may develop. In a majority of cases, after a shorter or longer period, bran not only ceases to relieve constipation, but sets up localized spasm in different segments of the colon, thus developing a secondary constipation which at times is difficult to cure. Without being able to offer concrete proof, it is held that this condition may lead to the development of malignant diseases [such as cancer]."

What have the manufacturers to say to such charges? That their own private experts tested bran on 22 *rats* and found that it did not injure them!

15. Agranulocytosis

MANY believe that in the field of foods and drugs, the Federal Food and Drugs Law prevents counterfeiting, at least of the type which involves serious health hazards. The case of All-Bran is that of a food product which jeopardizes the health of tens of thousands—perhaps hundreds of thousands—of persons and yet is completely beyond the control of Federal agencies; nor would it be controlled under the most drastic legislation which the politicians in charge of food and drug control have proposed as part of the "New Deal" program. When we turn to the field of drugs, we find a product responsible for a large number of deaths reported in the medical journals, yet sold absolutely without control and without the slightest warning to purchasers.

This product is amidopyrine, sold in the drug stores without prescription to anyone who asks for it, usually under the brand name of *Pyramidon.* Amidopyrine is often genuinely useful for the relief of headaches and pains, and it has been widely prescribed and recommended by physicians, who for a time considered it one of the least injurious of the common pain-relieving drugs. The number of those who bought it regularly without prescription grew rapidly, and the company selling Pyramidon built up a large and profitable business in it. (Ten tablets, costing five cents at wholesale, sell for 35 cents.)

A few years ago, however, it was discovered that amidopyrine and other chemically related drugs cause in some persons a blood ailment called agranulocytosis, characterized by a sharp decrease in the number of white corpuscles, those that protect the bloodstream against germ invasion. There have been hundreds of cases of this ailment, a great many of them fatal. It was also discovered that the number of cases had been increasing as the sale of amidopyrine, alone and in combination with other drugs, increased.

But if you go into a drug store today and ask for Pyramidon, it will be sold to you without question, exactly as it was sold before anyone knew that to some persons—and none can be sure in advance that he is not susceptible—it is a deadly poison. Iodine cannot be sold without a poison label; carbolic acid in many states is not sold without a prescription, and then it is prominently labeled "poison." But Pyramidon is sold without a trace of a warning of any kind which might interfere with its sale. Furthermore, not only is the public ignorant of the hazard, but many druggists know nothing about it, and some doctors who are too busy or too indifferent to read their medical journals are equally ignorant.

The makers of Pyramidon have this defense, though a feeble one: they do not advertise their product to the public, and they do not claim that it is safe. (They merely permit you to think it is safe, as a money counterfeiter permits you to think the bill he hands you is a genuine one.) But now we find advertisement after advertisement, in magazines and on billboards, of a new headache and pain remedy called Hexin, which contains amidopyrine. Said one advertisement for Hexin: "Originally developed for children . . . Hexin had to be gentle and safe." Other headache and pain remedies containing amidopyrine are Midol, Allonal, Amytal Compound, and Cibalgine.

DEATH IN THE MEDICINE CHEST

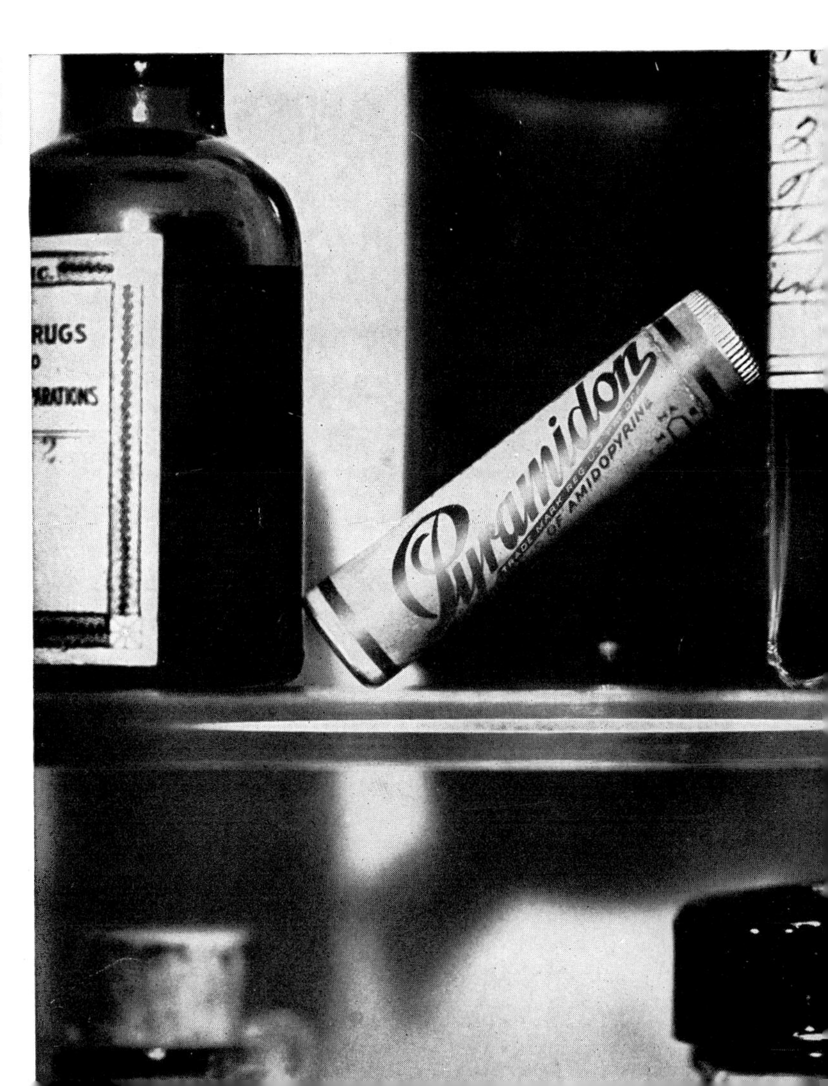

16. Poison

GOODS counterfeiters who deal in poisons frequently insist on the *corpus delicti.* Let anyone say that their products are dangerous and they immediately demand to see the bodies. In this class belong the makers of Pebeco toothpaste. Pebeco contains a poisonous chemical, potassium chlorate, and it so happens that potassium chlorate can kill and has killed people. "Potassium chlorate, yes. But not Pebeco," they say. And there you think you have them, for a German army officer once committed suicide by swallowing the contents of a tube of Pebeco. But again they have a comeback: "You don't eat Pebeco. You brush your teeth with it!"

The comeback is not so good as they think. In every tube of Pebeco there is about an ounce of potassium chlorate. A third of this would be a fatal dose to some adults, and a much smaller amount would be sufficient to kill young children. Babies frequently eat paint from furniture, and they have been known to drink kerosene and even to swallow the contents of a can of scouring powder. To such young gluttons, Pebeco would be a delightful dessert. And nowhere on the Pebeco tube or carton or in the scientific literature accompanying it are parents warned to keep this deadly poison out of the reach of children.

Even more important is the fact that users of Pebeco are not warned against swallowing some of the paste while using it in the ordinary way. And this brings up a question which, to consumers, is of far greater concern than the possibility of being killed outright by this or that food, drug, or cosmetic.

A third of an ounce of potassium chlorate is enough to kill. A tenth of an ounce is enough to make one very sick. What is the effect of a thousandth or a five-thousandth of an ounce? There are many who have been using Pebeco two or three times a day, day after day, for years. What is the effect on them of the repeated swallowing of tiny doses of a poison thousands of times? The impossibility of experimenting with human beings in large numbers, as one experiments with guinea pigs, prevents a positive answer to this question. And, because of this lack of experimental evidence, every manufacturer who makes money by selling poisons insists that small doses of *his* poison are harmless.

But all the consumer needs to know is that some authorities believe that small doses of poisons, continually repeated, may bring about degenerative changes in the body; may lead, especially in old age, to serious stomach, kidney, and other ailments; and may even shorten life. This applies not only to potassium chlorate but also to many other poisons which are regularly consumed with foods as well as with drugs, such as sodium benzoate, sulphur dioxide, lead, and arsenic. With such effects even a possibility, it is certainly wise to avoid every poison which does not, at least, serve some important function; and of all the poisons easy to avoid, the potassium chlorate in Pebeco is about the easiest.

IF YOU LIKE POISON

(There's an ounce of potassium chlorate—left-hand pile—in each tube of Pebeco. A third of an ounce—right-hand pile—is enough to kill)

17. That Hamburger

ONE special difference between money counterfeiting and goods counterfeiting should be pointed out. (There are, of course, many differences, most of which would probably establish money counterfeiting as a less serious crime, socially, than goods counterfeiting.) With money, the counterfeiting is encompassed in the original act of production. With goods, the counterfeiting—that is, the representation of the goods as something which it actually is not—may be introduced by the manufacturer or by a distributor; or the counterfeit may grow like a rolling snowball with the addition of new and more resplendent claims as the article progresses from manufacturer through distributors to consumer. Nationally advertised soaps, toothpastes, mouth washes, cosmetics, are counterfeits from the moment they leave the producers' hands. A druggist or a department store cosmetic clerk would need a brilliant imagination indeed to be able to improve upon the advertising agency's overwhelming descriptions of these products.

Sometimes, however, the entire job of counterfeiting is done by the retailer. Often the counterfeiter is a department store, a mail-order house, or a specialty shop. Here it is the butcher shop. Housewives will testify that many butchers turn counterfeiters every time they utter such a word as "tender" or "choice." Another kind of butcher-shop counterfeiting is practiced by many, though by no means all, butchers, with the aid of a chemical preservative called sodium sulphite. Stale, malodorous meat which a hungry dog would spurn, loses its foul odor, and turns a fresh, juicy red when dosed with sodium sulphite; and is frequently sold as good, fresh meat. Not only is the meat itself injurious, particularly if eaten rare, but the sodium sulphite is a poison which can do considerable injury to the digestive system. The meat most likely to be preserved (from the garbage can) with sodium sulphite is hamburger, simply because it is easy to make use of left-over and stale scraps by grinding them together with a dose of sulphite. If you must buy chopped meat, never (unless you have had long and happy association with your butcher) buy ready-prepared chopped meat. Order a cut and have it ground before your eyes.

Not only the butcher sins with sodium sulphite. At the hot-dog stand, the hamburger "palace," the restaurant or cafeteria you will often get this chemical with your hamburger sandwich.

Even if it wished, the Federal government could do nothing about such fraudulent sale of poisoned food by retailers, because interstate commerce is not involved. Some states confiscate sulphited meats when their inspectors find them, and occasionally levy small fines on the offenders. But they are interfering with an excellent source of profit. Successful state control of this evil is, therefore, exceptional.

THE CUSTOMER LIKES IT WITH MUSTARD
(the seller prefers sulphite)

18. Why Not Stork Oil?

This is the golden age of science.

Some day soon you may take up your favorite home magazine, unsuspectingly turn a page and there be confronted with an advertisement containing a picture something like the one below; and under the picture you may read:

"This is the only advertisement I shall ever write, for I am a scientist and not a writer, and I can spare no more time from my laboratory. But it is my duty personally to tell the women of America that my labors day and night for twenty-three years in their behalf have been finally crowned with success—with success far beyond my wildest imaginings in those early years of failure and discouragement. Only now, after the greatest laboratories and clinics in Europe and America have checked my findings to the last and most minute detail, can I say these words: 'By one year from today every woman

Professor Goocen-Gugenov in His Laboratory
(after years of painstaking research)

in the civilized world, whatever her age, can have a complexion equal to that of the greatest beauty now living.'

"There have been so many glowing promises, so many cherished hopes shattered, that women will find my simple statements difficult to believe. Therefore, I shall tell the story of my discovery briefly, in as plain, non-technical terms as possible. It is necessary to begin with my boyhood, at the time when my imagination was stirred by my newly gained knowledge of the importance of the stork in the history of the race. In later years, of course, I discovered that the stork was only a symbol, but my scientist's sixth sense told me that there must be a reason for this symbol. And then and there I vowed that I would not rest until I had resolved the mystery of the stork; until I had discovered whether there was not, within the graceful body of this winged creature, some property, some principle, some element which

Miss Celestine At Her Desk
("here's a formula that looks cheap")

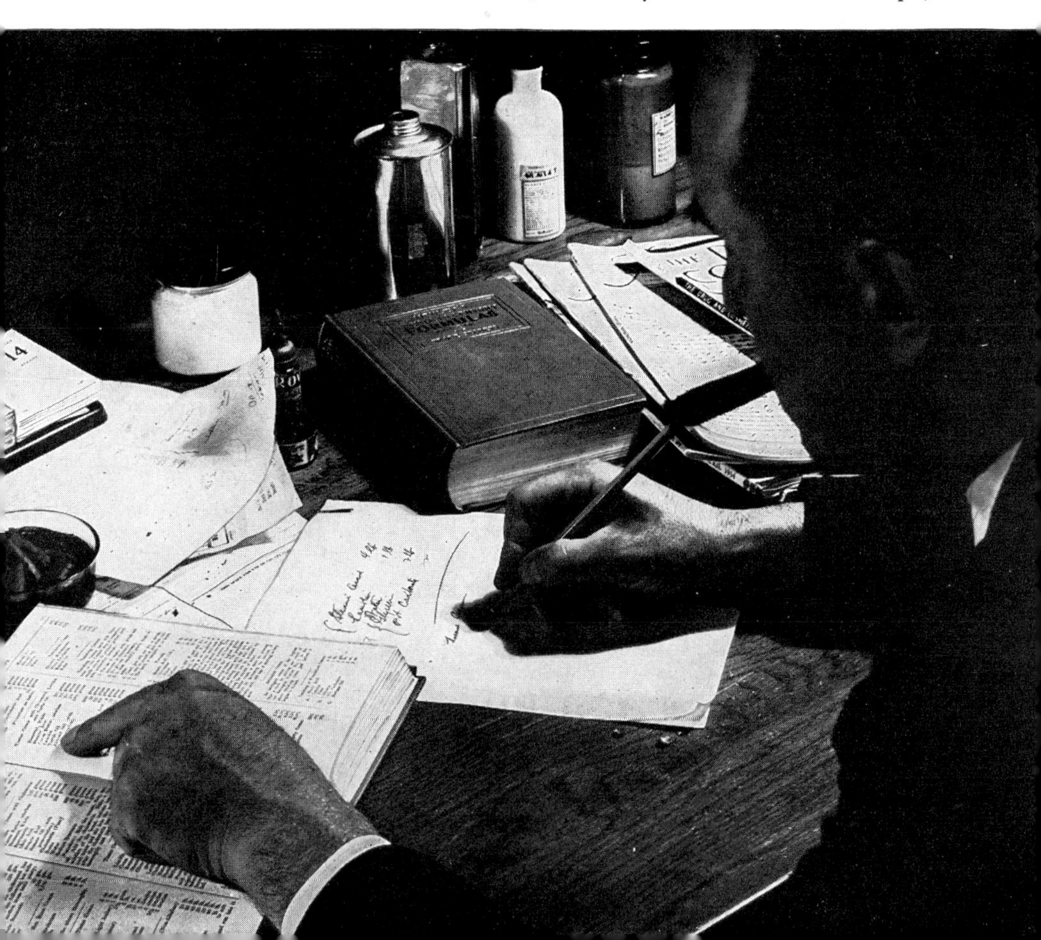

might give to grown women that perfection of skin possessed only by new-born babes, etc. And so, etc., etc. . . . Finally, Miss Celestine, my friend, who has herself won renown as a cosmetician, prevailed upon me to let her present this discovery to the world.

. . . .

"Miss Celestine announces with great pleasure that it is her honor and privilege to make available to the women of America Professor Googen-Gugenov's discovery. By special arrangement with leading department stores and exclusive shops, the original Stork Oil Alpha Ray Cream prepared by Professor Googen-Gugenov in his own laboratory is now available at twenty-five dollars the two-ounce jar."

Ah, Science!

The second picture shows the origin of such discoveries. "Speed" Jones, who is Miss Celestine, decided that a new product was necessary to put his waning cosmetic business back on its feet. He hired an advertising agency, a big and successful one, to map out a campaign. He looked up a few cold cream formulae in a standard formulary, got prices from a very ethical pharmaceutical house to see which was the cheapest (choosing one at three cents a jar), did some careful research with his nose to see what synthetic perfume he should use, got samples of expensive-looking jars (at a cost of four cents a jar), approved the advertising, placed his order with the pharmaceutical house, and got things humming. Two years later few remembered even the name of the great discovery, but it had netted him a hundred thousand dollars, and he was ready to launch a new cream with "ultra-violet hormones" in it.

Alas, Reality!

19. "Science Proves It"

As an example of the use of Science in advertising, consider the advertising campaign for ScotTissue and Waldorf toilet paper which enlivened home magazines a few years ago. Said the advertisements: "Science finds Harmful Acids . . . Mercury . . . Arsenic in many brands of Toilet Tissue. 660 Brands tested . . . 2 out of 3 found 'Unsafe . . . unfit to use.' . . . Recent tests in a hospital laboratory showed that 455 out of 660 brands of toilet tissue contain acids which may be extremely irritating in contact with mucous membrane. Some brands were actually found to contain unsafe quantities of wood splinters, injurious chemicals, mercury, aluminum, chlorine, even arsenic. . . . ScotTissue and Waldorf are two tissues that are medically safe, approved by doctors, hospitals and health authorities. . . . ScotTissue and Waldorf conformed to accepted medical standards of safety."

In view of the talk about "medical standards" and hospital tests, the Bureau of Investigation of the American Medical Association became interested, and attempted to obtain from the Scott Paper Company a statement of the basis for the claims. Only with difficulty was it learned that there actually was a scientist in the case—Dr. John A. Killian, Director of the Department of Biochemistry of the New York Post Graduate Medical School and Hospital. When Dr. Killian finally replied to the American Medical Association's letters, he failed, for some reason, to answer certain important questions. Then the Scott Company adopted the advertiser's usual method of reply—a visit from a representative of the company's advertising agency. The following is quoted from the A.M.A.'s story of the interview:

> "He admitted frankly that the advertising was exaggerated; and opined that if advertising was seventy per cent accurate, it was considered quite honest copy—otherwise it would lack the necessary emotional appeal. When the representative was asked for evidence supporting the statement that the product was made according to the standards of the medical profession, he replied that they had no evidence that this product complies with the 'standards of the medical profession.' "

Only after this visit did Dr. Killian send the A.M.A. a summary of the analyses of toilet papers. The analyses showed:

1. More than fifty-five percent of the 660 brands examined contained no more wood fibers than were found in ScotTissue and Waldorf.

2. Examination for bundles of splinters showed about four bundles per sheet for Waldorf and about one bundle in fifteen sheets for ScotTissue. But there were nine other brands with fewer splinters than ScotTissue, six of these brands having no splinters whatever.

3. Only 12 of the 660 brands contained arsenic, the maximum amount found being about one twenty-thousandth of a grain (about one ten-millionth of an ounce) per sheet.

Says the A.M.A.:

> "The statements regarding mercury were equally unsatisfactory. . . . On the question concerning the concentrations of arsenic that he considered deleterious or harmful, Dr. Killian replied that from his knowledge of the literature neither he nor, he believed, anyone else could answer the question. . . . Yet, on the basis of the work done by Dr. Killian, the Scott Paper Company have not hesitated to blazon from one end of the country to the other the implied claim that the American public is running risks of arsenic poisoning from the use of some brands of toilet paper!"

It should be noted that not only did Dr. Killian fail to repudiate publicly the gross falsification of his work by the company, but he also directly aided them in their counterfeiting by withholding information and evading questions of the A.M.A.

It cannot be too strongly emphasized that honest science and sales promotion do not mix. When a scientist, no matter of what rank or reputation, sells his opinions and his name to an advertiser, his opinions no longer merit acceptance by consumers. To a degree incredible to the layman, persons with scientific training but sound business instincts can prove practically anything. Is scientific proof ordered from a laboratory that Xtrafast Antiseptic will kill 40 billion bacteria in nine seconds flat? Proof is delivered with the aid of a strain of bacteria so weak that a mean look would almost finish them off. Is the advertising agency's order for proof that artichokes added to the diets of children will halve the number of their illnesses and give them sounder teeth? Proof is offered after experiments on children so undernourished that even lollipops would benefit them. By choosing the proper implements and conditions for the experiment and knowing precisely at what point to stop, the advertisers' scientific employees could prove that life on this planet is impossible without canned spinach, onions, apple butter, or California sunshine. The

"No Arsenic"
(nor in 648 other toilet papers)

head of a large commercial technical laboratory recently said (in private): "We work very close with our clients." That just about sums up the situation.

When advertisers employ scientists whose positions give them "news-value," their advertising is carried on partly in the news columns of the papers. News reports of alleged scientific discoveries should not, therefore, be accepted without question. If you should read some day about the discovery made by university professors that persons exposed to tuberculosis in air-conditioned rooms were not infected, you should only watch the advertisements to see whether the manufacturers of air-conditioning equipment are not making "scientific" preparations for their winter campaign.

In the field of nutrition, particularly, must "scientific" opinions be regarded with skepticism, since a large percentage of scientific workers in this field are on the payrolls of various food interests. Consciously or not, most of these research workers are strongly influenced by the fact that their work must show the "right" results, or they will lose their lucrative jobs. If they were completely honest scientists they would not impose upon the faith of consumers by failing to reveal their business connections when they publicize their paid-for opinions. Remember this when you read this or that famous professor's advice about milk, or ice cream, or sugar.

20. More Science

VAPEX is advertised as "A famous wartime discovery." Says one advertisement for this product: "Prominent medical research laboratory advises breathing Vapex because 1. The vapor penetrates to the real seat of a cold—the inner breathing passages. 2. Vapex has superior germ-killing power. Unbiased tests by a prominent medical research laboratory prove that the vapor of a single drop of Vapex kills dense colonies of germs present in head-colds. . . . Many cheaper imitations of Vapex are said to be 'just as good.' But science proves they are *not*. Vapex has a remarkable germ-killing power."

Famous wartime discovery? A shipment of Vapex was seized by the Federal Food and Drug Administration for misbranding. Upon analysis, it was found to be essentially alcohol, water, and volatile oils such as menthol and lavender oil. In other words, just one more menthol inhalant.

Says the government's "Notices of Judgment": "The statement . . . regarding the curative and therapeutic effect of the article, 'Laboratory tests have proved that the Vapex vapor kills the pathogenic

—AND MORE DISCOVERIES

FACIAL CREAM
PEPSODENT Junis FACIAL CREAM
A PEPSODENT PRODUCT
A discovery of dramatic promise
skin awakens
renewed lif
That's why women are thril
s such remarkable things
IT was not a beauty expert but a scientist who watched youth fade from women's skins and sought a way to check it.
"It may not work," he said, "but I'll put into a face cream the youthful substance old skins lack . . . and then we'll see what happens."
That's what he did. And today two million
million other women who have tried it. D
neglect an opportunity that has so much to
with charm and feminine allure. Send the cou
for a generous test supply today.
FREE—GENEROUS SUPP
PEPSODENT
Junis
FACIAL CREAM

bacteria present in the breathing passages' was false and fraudulent, since the article contained no ingredient or combination of ingredients capable of producing the effect claimed."

The company wisely did not contest the government's charges and the shipment was destroyed. Since each 75-cent bottle contains only a half-ounce of Vapex, costing the maker about two cents (most of that for alcohol), the destruction involved no great loss. One might, however, regret the destruction of a great deal of good glass, for the Vapex bottle, small though it is, is cleverly formed with a prodigious amount of glass to conceal the fact that the bottle contains only a tiny amount of fluid.

In Junis masterly research is typified. "Science has discovered a new principle in skin care. . . . Skin contains a natural softening substance which makes it fresh, alluring—glamorous. The scientist got some of this natural substance in pure form [what scientist?]. He put it into the finest facial cream he could develop. Women tried it and their skins grew clearer, more transparent. Age lines melted into the soft curves of youth. Skin began to stir with life. The natural skin-softening substance put into Junis Cream the scientist named *sebisol*. Sebisol is our name for this part of the chemical substance of your own skin. It is essential to every living cell. It is so rare [what, no living cells?] we searched throughout the world for a sufficient supply." If this were one-hundreth part true, it would be one of the great scientific discoveries of the last five hundred years, and women all over the world would be erecting altars to the "discoverer" of sebisol. But like other examples of the cosmetic industry's masterly research, it will supply good advertising copy for a few years, after which it will join the ranks of a thousand other great "discoveries" that first saw the light of day in an advertising agency.

The last example of science in business speaks for itself—Statler Toilet Tissue. "Protect Your Health. Ultra Violet Rayed."

PREVENTIVE MEDICINE UP-TO-DATE

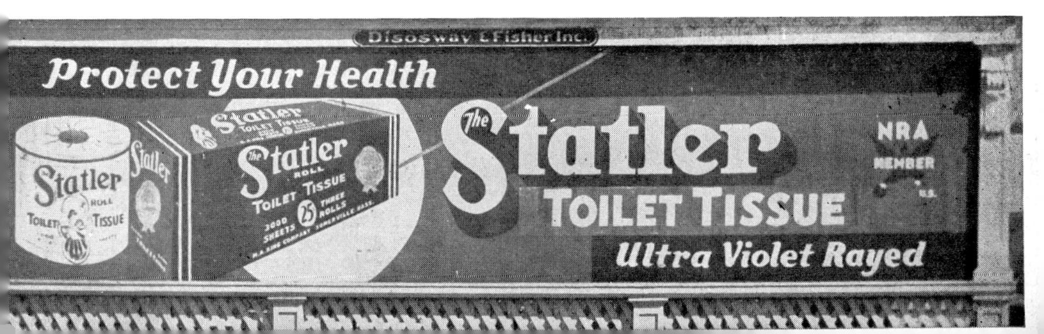

21. Vitamin D

Business is interested in honest scientific achievement if it has "practical" value—that is, if it can be translated into dividends. Scientists, not of the advertising agency variety, discovered that a deficiency of vitamin D in the diets of young children, combined with lack of sunlight, caused rickets and also hindered the proper development of the teeth. The disease could be avoided or cured by giving the children cod liver oil, which is rich in vitamin D.

The "practical" value of this knowledge, except to a few drug producers, was comparatively slight. Later a method was found for concentrating the vitamins of the unpalatable oil in little tablets. Here was a *practical* opportunity. The ethical Squibb Company and other companies quickly discovered that everyone, children and adults, needed the vitamins of cod liver oil and should be taking vitamin tablets. This, despite the absence of proof that adults (except perhaps for pregnant women and nursing mothers) who eat a well-balanced diet need artificial supplies of vitamins. And the exploitation of vitamins by Squibb and others continued even when it was discovered that an excess of vitamin D could be injurious to health.

Then along came an even more "practical" discovery—a method of putting artificially produced vitamin D into all kinds of foods. The photographs show some of the types of food to which vitamin D is now being added. The list includes a great many brands of pasteurized milk and of evaporated milk, many brands of bread, ice cream, and some prepared vegetables for infants; and it is even rumored that vitamin D is going to be added to hot dogs! Here, then, is an example of the use of science in a profit economy. Vitamin D in excess is a health hazard. Children who get plenty of sunlight don't need any added to their normal diets, at least during the summer months. They often get it anyway in cod liver oil; and now, for the sake of profits, they get it also in milk, bread, and other foods.

Naturally, knowledge of the harmful effects of excess amounts of vitamin D is suppressed. The breakfast cereal manufacturers provide another example of the suppression of vital information which might interfere with sales and profits. Each brand of cereal, the advertisements show, will build up children, end their nervousness, give them good marks in school, etc., etc. But every cereal advertiser suppresses the fact that, in the opinion of competent investigators, cereals in excess interfere with the proper development of children's teeth.

...y Are Children
...r Sick?

The Sunshine Vitamin *(it shines on dividend days)*

22. Ear Oil

In the pages that follow, specific advertisements will be discussed, chiefly to indicate to the reader how advertising for products which he may consider buying should be analyzed. Frequently the advertised claims will be sufficient to brand a product as counterfeit without any need for examining the product itself. Surely one who has lost his hearing but not his intelligence does not need to buy a bottle of Leonard Ear Oil to know that it is counterfeit, if he examines the Ear Oil advertisement which appears on the druggist's wrapper. A moment's reflection will show that the claim that "Leonard Ear Oil relieves both Head Noises and Deafness" is a fraud, since no oil rubbed behind the ears or inserted in the nostrils can mend a broken eardrum or restore dead nerves.

This counterfeit claim is exceptional only in its obviousness. If you will pick up any women's magazine and read the advertisements, or examine car-cards and billboards, or claims made over the radio, you will find yourself wallowing in an ocean of "ear oil," though the copy-writer's cleverness may cause you difficulty in recognizing it as such.

Since nearly all advertising intended for the ultimate consumer is false, misleading, or exaggerated, there is only one safe way for a consumer without technical knowledge of the product advertised to approach an advertisement: that is, with the assumption that it is false, misleading, or exaggerated. The ear oil claims are an example of completely *false* advertising. A large percentage of all advertising is simply *misleading*. An advertisement may not contain a single expressed untruth, but it diverts your attention from the essential facts as to quality or safety, and seeks to leave you with the *impression* that the product is of superlative desirability as compared with all other products of its class or price range, with no faults whatsoever. A very large percentage of department store advertising is of this type. Typical advertising *exaggeration* is found in the claims for some "health" foods. In the hands of expert copy-writers, a food with a slight nutritional value can become a panacea.

If you approach advertising with a great deal of skepticism, you will find it less difficult to spot counterfeit claims and implications than if you start with the assumption that an advertisement must be honest because it carries a respectable name or appears in a respectable publication.

Name ....

Address ....

Date .... *Charges* ....

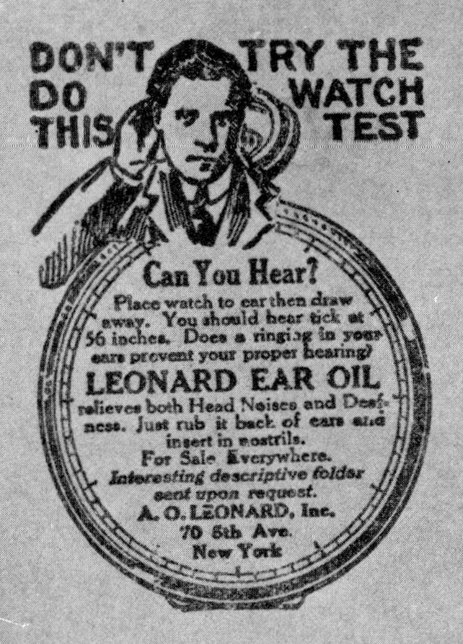

Also excellent for Temporary Deafness caused by Flu, Colds, Swimming, etc.

Get a Bottle To-Day

Price $1.25

Read what users say on other side.

Ear Oil?

(banana oil!)

23. Gas

EMERGENCY action in every drop," "99,000,000 foot-pounds per gallon," "Socony Means Quality and Service," "Pep Makes a Winner," "SuperShell is Supercharged," "Guarantees Smoother Performance." Such are the advertised claims by which the gasoline producers try to get your business.

"Emergency Action in every drop." What is emergency action? "Guarantees Smoother Performance." Smoother than what? And what about that 99,000,000 foot-pounds per gallon? Is this an advertiser's conception of a theoretical atomic energy, and if so, of what slightest consequence is it to the driver of an automobile with an internal combustion engine?

As a matter of fact, these claims, intended to influence you to believe that each gasoline is the best, are mere attention-catchers, and are worthless as a means of helping you decide which gasoline will give the most satisfactory and economical performance in your car. And this despite the fact that gasoline is in no sense "ear oil." It is an absolutely essential product, completely devoid of style factors, with measurable and comparable qualities.

When the United States government wants to buy gasoline you can be sure it does not send out an office boy to look for gasoline billboards in order to learn which popular brand of gasoline is best. It prepares a technical specification based upon such factors as octane rating (anti-knock characteristics), ease of starting, ease of acceleration, crank-case oil dilution, and corrosive properties. These factors are expressed in figures and physical units. For example, to assure ease of starting, the government specification requires that a certain percentage of the gasoline shall vaporize at or below a fixed low temperature. Gasoline refiners are then permitted to bid on the specification, and the lowest price gets the business. The specification includes no reference to emergency action or winning pep.

The individual consumer cannot, of course, buy by specification and competitive bidding, but he could learn to use information about available brands of gasoline which would be more enlightening than "SuperShell is Supercharged"—such information, for example, as that contained in a Consumers' Research report on gasoline:

"*Shell Supercharge* Regular Grade. . . . Octane number 72—above average. Ease of starting and acceleration better than average. Among worst in tendency to vapor lock."

If advertising were intended to be informing rather than misleading, this is how a gasoline billboard might read (but won't):

Universal Gasoline sold in this county is certified by U. S. Government Approved Testing Laboratory No. 19 to meet the following grades:

GENERAL GRADE	A
Octane rating	70
Ease of Starting	A
Acceleration	A
Crankcase Oil Dilution	B
Corrosion	A
Gum Formation	B
Vapor Lock	C

Contains no lead.

Automobile owners would quickly learn the relative importance of each of these grades in the operation of their automobiles.

99,000,000 FOOT-POUNDS
(an advertiser gets down to facts and figures)

24. Perfection

If you buy a toilet soap or a pair of stockings because the advertisements failed to give you essential information, the damage can be repaired. If the soap irritates your skin, you can buy another brand next time. If the stockings wear poorly, you can experiment with another brand. But suppose the advertiser's failure to give essential information—the need for which may not even occur to you—leads you to buy costly mechanical equipment such as an oil burner, a refrigerator, a washing machine or a vacuum cleaner, supposed to last for many years? Then your error is costly indeed.

The advertising for the General Electric Oil Furnace has been chosen for discussion not because of any deficiencies in this burner, but because its manufacturer is able to purchase materials and supplies on exact and full specifications, and industrial concerns buying many of this company's products are able to obtain essential information. But necessary data are not given to the ultimate consumer.

"They had perfected a complete, coordinated heating unit," says one advertisement for the General Electric Oil Furnace. Perfected? The consumer should be given such information as the following, so that he can judge the degree of perfection for himself:

How many service calls have there been per year per thousand installations?
What is the average number of hours per year furnaces have been out of service because of breakdowns and repairs?
How many explosions or fires have there been per thousand installations?
What is the percentage efficiency of the burner and how does this compare with the efficiencies of other burners?
What is the life of the burner as evidenced by a clear guarantee to replace major parts without cost during that period?

Says another advertisement, "Many former hand-fired furnace owners report [fuel] savings up to 50%." This figure is meaningless without the following additional information:

At what price of oil and what price of coal are the comparisons made?
What changes have there been in the price of the grade of oil used during the past five years and what is the present trend?
How much electric current is used to run the furnace?
Is it necessary to spend extra money for insulating the house or for new radiators or valves to make the estimated savings?
What about repair costs, interest on the cost of the furnace, and an annual

THE G-E OIL FURNACE DIFFERS FROM AN "OIL BURNER"...

as a Skyscraper differs from a Grass Hut

BE FAIR TO YOURSELF SEE THE G-E

NO "ATTACHMENT BURNER" can give you what the G-E Oil Furnace does.

What you might save on first cost with an attachment, you throw away on operating cost and maintenance. 19% of all G-E Oil Furnace owners formerly had attachment burners. Many owners report 25% average fuel saving with the G-E Oil Furnace over an attachment. Many former hand-fired furnace owners report savings up to 50%.

Of course, you don't buy oil heat for economy alone, and with the G-E Oil Furnace you get far more than just that. Heating and year-round hot water become as automatic as an electric light.

All because the G-E is a complete, coordinated unit, with a dozen exclusive features that no other equipment can offer.

Before you decide on any kind of automatic heat, ask yourself if it can give you what the G-E Oil Furnace does. See the G-E at the showroom—or at least write or phone *and find out how you can have this furnace now for 10% down, no more to pay until September.*

General Electric Company
Air Conditioning Department, Div. AH8
570 Lexington Ave., New York, N. Y.

I want more information about the G-E Oil Furnace—*free.*

Name..........
Residence..........
City & State..........

GENERAL ELECTRIC OIL FURNACE

G-E AIR CONDITIONING FOR WINTER, SUMMER AND YEAR ROUND

THE AMERICAN HOME, AUGUST, 1934 129

THE "HOUSE OF MAGIC" TALKS ABOUT ECONOMY

allowance for depreciation? (Interest, depreciation, and repairs over a period of years might amount to more than $100 annually.)

Many oil-burner owners have experienced difficulty in getting the proper grade of oil when they needed it; in getting prompt servicing (this is important in cold midwinter) even when servicing is guaranteed. What assurances has the purchaser in these respects?

Such is the information the consumer needs—but does not get.

25. Clothes Counterfeit

ON THE opposite page is a typical clothing advertisement—typical, in that it provides almost no information by which the quality of the suits can be judged. In the entire advertisement there is only one word that conveys any definite meaning concerning quality. The word is "worsted," which means that the suits are all-wool. But even that does not tell you what percentage of the wool is reworked, short-fiber wool, which weakens the fabric and shortens the life of the garment. Nor can you determine from the advertisement whether the seams will pull loose or the lining wear out long before the fabric. If you are one of those fortunates who can afford to buy a new suit every few months without cutting down on other purchases, then these things will not matter. You can be content if the style and appearance of the fabric satisfy you. But to most people the wearing out of clothing within a few months means a serious loss.

Inspection of a garment will help you little more than reading the advertisement. But the manufacturer or the seller could give you information telling you what you need to know.* He could, that is, if he were not a counterfeiter. An advertisement for a suit, a dress, a coat, a shirt, in fact, for any kind of textile product, should tell you the tensile strength (resistance to tearing), and the abrasive strength (resistance to rubbing)—both determinable by simple, standard tests—the effects of standard cleaning and washing tests on strength, color and size, the effects of light, and other factors which are important for different kinds of garments and fabrics.

But the manufacturers find it more profitable to let you think you are getting perfection. What they often give you is thus described by Professor Pauline Beery Mack, a textile authority:

"It has been shown by various researches that the following tricks of the trade are practiced in the ready-made garment industries: Workmanship at places easily seen is sometimes good, while seams and other concealed parts may be sewed with inferior thread and finished in such a careless manner as to make for poor durability. Weighted silk linings, or linings of rayons which cannot withstand abrasion, are frequently placed in garments the exterior of which far outwears the lining. Weighted silk is frequently used as a trimming on woolen or pure silk garments, and wears out before the garment proper is ready to be discarded.

---

* (See page 90.)

"Men's shirts are often made of a broadcloth which has a very heavy appearance, but which has a low breaking strength in the crosswise direction. . . . Shirts are known to have been sold with a 'pre-shrunk' label on the inside of the collar band when only this part of the garment has been given a pre-shrinking treatment. . . .

"Men's underwear may possess neither strength nor resistance to shrinking, and nationally advertised brands are as unreliable in this regard as other brands. In some nationally advertised brands, different fabrics, all of the same general appearance, have been used in different garments, with nothing to indicate to the buyer what he is getting."

(from the New York *Times,* September 3, 1934.)

At Least They Tell You It's Wool

26. Eat It Like Candy

An illuminating example of the kind of information which advertisers give as contrasted with the kind of information suppressed is afforded by examination of the advertisement for Ex-Lax, a chocolate laxative containing the drug phenolphthalein (Feen-A-Mint, a laxative gum, Cascarets, and Espotabs, all widely advertised, also contain phenolphthalein), followed by the reading of this statement concerning phenophthalein laxatives by Dr. J. F. Montague, in a book that every cathartic addict should read, *I Know Just the Thing for That:**

"Perhaps you can scarcely believe that in this day and age a substance which is poisonous is being used for its laxative effect, yet we find that phenolphthalein, which is a definite poison, is actually being used in literally hundreds of patent medicine preparations sold for laxative purposes. . . .

"Like most poisons, it can be harmless if taken in small doses at long intervals. However, all people are not alike in their ability to tolerate this poison even in small amounts and the reactions which are produced by taking it vary from a skin eruption to a severe kidney irritation. It must stand to reason that if in very small doses severe physical reaction can be produced, the constant repetition of these doses of poison will damage the system to an even greater extent. Indeed, several deaths have been directly attributed to the taking of this drug. . . . Some of the most severe cases of spastic colitis I have ever seen have been due to the prolonged use of phenolphthalein cathartics.

"It may with truth be argued that an overdose of any medicine is likely to have disastrous results and that we should not condemn it because the directions which accompanied it were not followed. In the cases where an overdose was taken such reasoning may apply. However, when the laxatives containing phenolphthalein were taken precisely as the printed label directed, yet severe skin rashes, loss of the nails, sores in mouth and nose, and even grave kidney diseases resulted, this alibi for the manufacturers does not hold.

" . . . The 'candy laxative' is in itself a bad thing because it helps and encourages the formation of a 'laxative habit' in early life, which the unfortunate individual may retain when grown up. When this

* The John Day Company, New York.

'candy' is employed to camouflage a deadly poison, its unrestricted employment becomes little less than a crime."

Here are a few

DON'TS

about laxatives!

Don't take a laxative that is too strong—that shocks the system—that weakens you!

Don't take a laxative that is offered as a cure-all—a treatment for a thousand ills!

Don't take a laxative where you have to keep on increasing the dose to get results!

TAKE EX-LAX—THE LAXATIVE THAT DOES NOT FORM A HABIT

You take Ex-Lax just when you need a laxative—it won't form a habit. You don't have to keep on increasing the dose to get results. Ex-Lax is effective—but it is mild. Ex-Lax doesn't force—it acts gently yet thoroughly. It works over-night without over-action.

Children like to take Ex-Lax because they love its delicious chocolate taste. Grown-ups, too, prefer to take Ex-Lax because they have found it to be thoroughly effective—without the disagreeable after-effects of harsh, nasty-tasting laxatives.

For 28 years, Ex-Lax has had the confidence of doctors, nurses, druggists and the general public alike, because it is everything a laxative should be.

At any drug store—in 10c and 25c boxes.

WATCH OUT FOR IMITATIONS!

Ex-Lax has stood the test of time. It has been America's favorite laxative for 28 years. Insist on genuine Ex-Lax—spelled E-X-L-A-X—to make sure of getting Ex-Lax results.

Keep "regular" with

EX-LAX

THE CHOCOLATED LAXATIVE

(from Hearst's *International-Cosmopolitan,* November, 1934.)

NOT ENOUGH "DONT'S"

27. Testimonials

ARE testimonials also counterfeit? Read the advertisement opposite, and then read the following from a letter to the American Medical Association written by the Dean of the Vienna Medical Faculty:

"It has been brought to the attention of the Vienna Medical Faculty that medical testimonials favoring one of the yeast preparations placed on the market by the Fleischmann Yeast Company in New York have been placed at the disposal of this company by certain members of the medical faculty in Vienna, and that these testimonials are spread and misused . . . in quack-fashion. Even though the testifiers in question cannot personally be responsible, . . . the Vienna Medical Faculty instituted an extensive inquiry. . . .

". . . not a single member of the Board of Professors (heads of departments) of the medical faculty is involved in this affair. Seven *privatdozents* not included on the board, and not one of whom either has the official position of teacher or is in charge of a department, are concerned here."

As for the claims allegedly supported by the testimonializers, note the following from the Medical Association's *Journal:* "That it [yeast] is of much value in . . . acne or furunculosis is doubtful, as many patients who keep on suffering from these conditions in spite of liberal ingestion of yeast are willing to testify. That among the host of persons taking yeast a skin disorder clears up occasionally is not surprising. The association might be entirely accidental."

The Fleischmann Company is now out-testimonializing itself in a campaign for a "new strain" of yeast. It is significant that the company does not divulge the names of the laboratories or the scientists responsible for the discovery, or the names of the great European and American clinics where the new yeast was said to have been tested. The "new strain" is probably, as usual, on the consumer.

The cigarette companies also use testimonials. But read the following from a letter published in *Advertising and Selling:*

> "My sixteen-year-old son came to me the other day asking 'how come' and pointed to a full-page Camel ad showing Ellsworth Vines holding a cigarette in his hand. . . . The entire ad is so worded that one must believe Ellsworth Vines smokes Camels.
>
> "My son then showed me an interview with Ellsworth Vines in *The Open Road for Boys*, one paragraph of which reads as follows:
>
> " 'As to my habits, I don't smoke except, perhaps, that once in four or five months I may have a pipe of tobacco, or a cigar. . . .' "

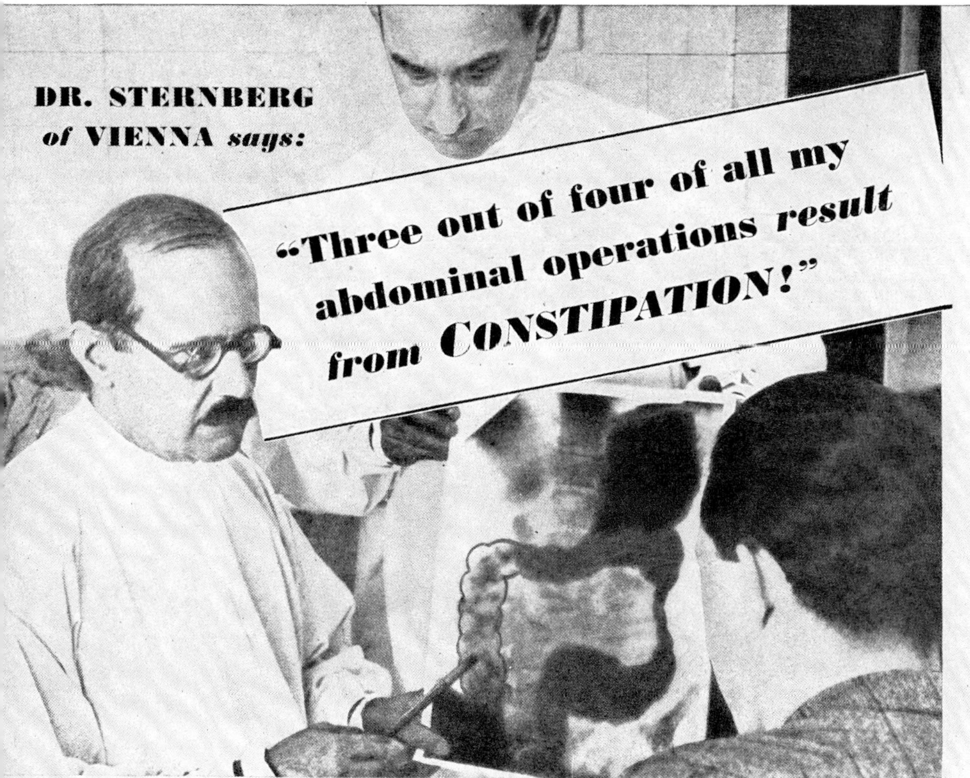

DR. STERNBERG (*pointing to X-ray*), *says, "The poisons caused by constipation seep into the blood . . . cause grave disturbances." He strongly recommends eating yeast.**

HE following statement is by Dr. Julius ›ternberg, head of the First Surgical : of the well-known Mariahilfer Hospital enna, Austria. Dr. Sternberg says:—

fter many years' experience . . . I can with certainty that three-fourths of all bdominal operation cases that come be- ne are a direct or indirect consequence nstipation. *Constipation may be the cause colitis, hemorrhoids, appen- s, even peritonitis.*"

n constipation be cured? Dr. berg goes on to explain:—

"Cathartics and laxative drugs ı . . . irritate the intestines . . . What ed is a method which will soften the ts of the intestines and stimulate nor- tion. *Such a simple, natural method is the of fresh yeast.*"

ı tire quickly—if your complex- bad—if you have frequent indi- n after meals—you are very likely ng from a stagnant condition of ntestinal tract.

l in all probability all that's l to banish this condition is to sh yeast! If you will add Fleischmann's Yeast to your diet and eat it regularly, you can prove this to your own satisfaction.

So try it now. Yeast will "tone" your intestines —*strengthen* them. Then, as your bowels act to cleanse your system of harmful waste matter every day, notice how your strength picks up . . . how much better your meals digest . . . how much less often you are troubled with headaches, bad skin, bad breath, sore throats, colds.

It's so simple! Just eat 3 cakes of Fleischmann's fresh Yeast each day, faithfully—before meals, or between meals and at bedtime—plain, or dissolved in a third of a glass of water.

You can get Fleischmann's Yeast at grocers, restaurants, soda fountains. Start eating it today.

DR. G. FAROY, of Paris, author of the well-known "Digestive Therapeutics" (1928), states: "I advise patients to avoid cathartics . . . I know no safer means of correcting constipation than fresh yeast."

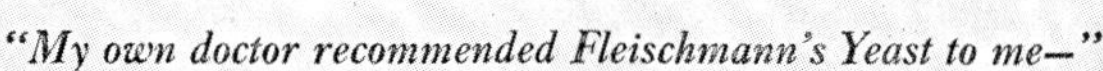

"I am a teacher," *writes* Mrs. Irene Clarence *of New York,* "and I was very discouraged because for years I had been suffering from constipation and stomach trouble and had tried all sorts of pills and medicines, laxatives and cathartics without avail. I was afraid that I'd have to give up my work altogether.

"A doctor friend of mine recommended Fleischmann's Yeast and I ate it regularly. Results were astonishingly good. My elimination became regular and I found I could eat anything without ensuing distress . . . I had no more use for 'remedies' . . . And the yeast cleared up my complexion, too."

**Important!*

Fleischmann's Yeast for health comes only in the foil-wrapped cake with the yellow label. It's yeast in its fresh, effective form—rich in health-giving vitamins B, G and D—the kind famous doctors recommend. Write for booklet. Dept. Y-E-4, Standard Brands Inc., 691 Washington St., New York City.

(from *Delineator,* April, 1933.)

DR. STERNBERG RECOMMENDS

28. Good Housekeeping Approves

IT IS the definite policy of Good Housekeeping to make its advertising pages trustworthy and reliable. EVERY product advertised in Good Housekeeping is guaranteed."

This statement appears in every issue of *Good Housekeeping.* There is a reference to it on almost every page containing advertisements. Is it an honest guarantee, or would the consumer be justified in believing that it is simply a means used by *Good Housekeeping* to get more advertising contracts by helping goods counterfeiters to "pass" their counterfeit products? You can judge for yourself from the following brief analysis of a few typical products guaranteed by this Hearst publication:

Flit: Advertised in *Good Housekeeping* as a mothproofing spray. No mothproofing spray can be relied upon, and dependence on Flit may cause the ruin of expensive woolen garments.

Listerine: Advertised in *Good Housekeeping* as a preventive of pneumonia and tuberculosis! (See page 28 concerning mouth washes.)

Lysol: Advertised in *Good Housekeeping* for "feminine hygiene." Lysol is a satisfactory disinfectant for floors and plumbing, but its use on delicate tissues especially as recommended is decidedly hazardous. See page 68 in connection with testimonials of the type Lysol uses.

Vick's Vatro-Nol—Vick's and *Good Housekeeping's* super-scientists (also the Bayer, Mistol, Listerine, Pepsodent Antiseptic, etc., scientists) have discovered how to prevent and cure colds. If only they would tell the ordinary research workers at Johns Hopkins about it!

Ambrosia: Good Housekeeping has tested Ambrosia in its own private laboratories and apparently found scientific support for the claim that one woman "Looks 20 . . . is 40" because she used Ambrosia, and that "You, too, can have a youthful skin that others envy" by using Ambrosia. The scientists of *Good Housekeeping* seem not to have been disturbed by the presence of carbolic acid in Ambrosia, though the New Hampshire State Board of Health condemned the product because of this dangerous ingredient.

Woodbury's Soap: See pages 24 and 25. *Vapex:* See page 54.

Grayban: Said one of the first "Grayban" advertisements: "A great scientist discovers how to bring back natural color to gray hair. The *same* golden liquid renews the color of blond, brown, black, or auburn hair . . . without the use of dangerous dye. . . . Only harmless ingredients used for skin and scalp disorders are combined in a neutral golden fluid to bring back all the youthful beauty of your hair coloring . . . Grayban, the miracle of science." The advertisement also informs you that Grayban has been tested and approved

	Page
othing, Shoes, Etc.	
tions	232
ernity Clothes	227
wear	184
ts' Wear	See Baby
)ressings	228
nity Frocks	214
	204
	249
ibber Co.	215

YOUR GUARANTY

IT IS the definite policy of Good Housekeeping to make its advertising pages trustworthy and reliable. EVERY product advertised in Good Housekeeping is guaranteed.

Paints, Varnishes & Oth
Johnson's Glo-Coat
Johnson's Wax
Liquid Veneer
Plastic Wood
Pratt & Lambert—"61" Varnish
Sherwin-Williams Paints
Simoniz & Simoniz Kleener
Valspar Enamels

by *Good Housekeeping* Bureau. The American Medical Association tested Grayban and reported that this discovery of a "great scientist" was just "another one of the bismuth hair dyes. Formulas for hair dyes having some salt of bismuth as the chief ingredient appear in most books of formulas for hair dyes and such products have been known for years." And the claim that it would restore the natural color to any hair was found to be just pure bunk.

Forhan's toothpaste (also Pepsodent, Colgate's, Ipana, and other toothpastes). *Good Housekeeping* has tested them and found that they actually will prevent pink toothbrush, remove 7 stains, and make you popular, etc., etc. If dental authorities (except *Good Housekeeping's* scientists) are agreed on any one thing, it is that no toothpaste or powder safe for daily use will prevent or cure bleeding gums, make teeth white, etc., etc.

Good Housekeeping has also approved Oyloff Dry Shampoo, advertised as an "amazing new liquid." This amazing liquid, selling for a dollar a bottle, proved, on analysis, to consist essentially of a colored and perfumed solution of salt water.

29. They Scrutinize

PERHAPS you will feel that if you can't trust the advertising in *Good Housekeeping* then you can't trust it in any popular magazine. You will be right. But what about newspapers? We can do no better than to examine the advertising in that Gibraltar of journalism, the New York *Times*. If other papers carry counterfeit advertising that is presumed to be your lookout. But the New York *Times* professes to be your sentinel. It says: "Advertisements in the New York Times are subject to scrutiny. A large volume of advertising is excluded yearly from The Times because it does not meet The Times standards." Is this also a helping hand to the goods-counterfeiters? Judge for yourself:

Kellogg's All-Bran—Advertised as a health food—see page 40

Pluto Water—The *Times* advertisement says "Avoid Laxatives that *Constipate* you! Physicians Warn Against Irritating Drugs." But Pluto Water is essentially a mixture of Epsom and Glauber's salts in water, and, like any other salt laxative, when used frequently it is constipating and irritating.

Phillips' Milk of Magnesia—Have you nervousness, neuralgia, auto-intoxication, frequent headaches, feeling of weakness, loss of appetite, indigestion, nausea, sleeplessness, mouth acidity, sour stomach? If you have, says the advertisement in the New York

FIT TO PRINT

Times, just take six teaspoonfuls of Phillips' Milk of Magnesia every day, and your troubles are at an end. This is plain, ordinary quackery, and dangerous to boot, for many will try to treat serious ailments, even stomach ulcers and cancer, with a laxative, after self-diagnosis encouraged by this kind of advertising.

Calox (The "Forgotten 60" toothpowder)—The New York *Times* presents this marvelous dentifrice that is going to do just about everything that all the other toothpaste and toothpowder advertisers have thought of. See page 26.

Bell-Ans—"I eat what I like and take Bell-Ans when food disagrees. . . . Gives prompt relief even in severe cases [of indigestion]." More quackery, encouraging dependence on an ordinary nostrum for what may prove to be serious ailments.

Bayer's Aspirin—Careful scrutiny by the *Times'* scrutinizers apparently revealed nothing wrong with Bayer advertising, although the Federal Trade Commission has found a great deal wrong with it, and for the benefit of Bayer's competitors has ordered the Bayer company to stop making claims—including the claim that aspirin is harmless—which have appeared in the *Times*.

Adex—We read in the *Times* that everyone should take it regularly. See page 56 concerning Vitamin D.

Delv—Says the *Times* advertisement: "A truly revolutionary advance in beauty science. Primrose House has spent years searching for some ingredient to duplicate the natural oil of the skin and its rejuvenating effect. . . ." No comment necessary.

A large number of other products which have been advertised in the *Times* could be cited, such as Montecatini Crystals with their marvelous ionic action, Elizabeth Arden's Gland Cream ($10), Siroil (which encourages self-medication for a condition which requires competent diagnosis and treatment), Eyelash Cream (which makes lashes long, dark, and luxuriant), Ipana toothpaste (for your poor bleeding gums), and Joyz' Maté ("Do you fear the dangerous age?").

In justice to the New York *Times* it should be said that it carries less objectionable advertising than most newspapers. By comparison with the Hearst papers,* for instance, the *Times* is a model of purity. But other papers boast no scrutinizers.

---

* The Hearst papers are outstanding examples of the general practice of *news* counterfeiting; but that is another story.

30. How To Get Advertising

With advertising providing the major part of their income, newspapers and magazines have developed many methods of aiding and abetting the advertisers. One of the most successful methods is that of concealing advertising in the columns devoted to reading matter. Consumers are beginning to read advertisements with varying degrees of defensive skepticism, but this armor is usually laid aside when news columns of papers and articles in magazines are being read (just as one would not be expecting to get a counterfeit bill when drawing money out of a bank). The job of convincing the reader that the counterfeit is pure gold thus becomes much simpler. Such concealed advertising is usually not paid for in cash, but is a form of bribery used to get contracts for paid advertising.

In women's and home magazines this bribery often takes the form of scientific articles by Ph.D.'s proving with impressive tables, charts, and photomicrographs that advertised brands of soaps or canned goods or cosmetics are always and invariably infinitely superior to non-advertised brands. In newspapers, the bribery may be more direct. There may be shopping columns in which the great bargains and superior quality of merchandise at certain stores is described. Some papers regularly give whole pages as bribes to advertisers, as in the real estate, automobile, and theatrical sections.

Another example is the "Foods and Diets Suggestions" section run weekly in *The New York Post*, which, through a recent change of ownership, became a friend of the common man and a foe to the shady practices of the bankers and the politicians. At the bottom of the section each week is a group of small advertisements for various food, beverage, and other products. And every week, Daniel R. Hodgdon, Ph.D., D.Sc., D.D., LL.D., writes scientific articles which often happen to promote the advertisers' sales. Of course, Dr. Hodgdon does not name the products. That is done in a news column. Thus, adjoining an advertisement of a Schultz product, is a learned article by Dr. Hodgdon about the simply amazing health-promoting properties of ginger ale, provided it is not one of the "cheap, adulterated, worthless products of the type that are flooding the market." In the next column is a "news" story about the costly, pure, and valuable ingredients used in its ginger ale by the Carl H. Schultz Company, 118 North Eleventh Street, Brooklyn. On another day, over an advertisement for H-B Cough Drops is a scientific article by Dr. Hodg-

JOURNALISM LENDS A HAND
(for value received)

don pointing out, quite truthfully, the worthlessness of vitamin A as an ingredient of cough drops (it's in Smith Brothers' drops—one of H-B's competitors), and alongside is a "news" story telling why workers in the H-B plant never have raw throats.

31. Analyzing Saráka

How a Consumer with Some Knowledge of Advertising Practices but no Knowledge of the Product Might Analyze the Advertising for Saráka:

TESTS by 15,862 doctors prove Saráka ideal for constipation." This statement, in the absence of some explanation of these tests, can be appraised only in the light of methods which have been used in preparing similar campaigns for other products. The following is the method which might be used by a manufacturer to lay a basis for a claim like this: samples are sent to all or most of the 160,000 physicians in the United States. With each sample goes an offer of more samples *and* a genuine alligator wallet or a $5 fountain pen ("with your name in gold") if the doctor will sign and return the enclosed form card stating that he *wishes to have more samples to test.* The number of doctors replying would be a good measure of the number of doctors wanting a free wallet or a fountain pen, but it would prove nothing with respect to tests of the laxative itself. Furthermore, the testing of a laxative is a job for a gastro-intestinal specialist, and there are not 15,000 nor even 5,000 of these in the United States. If there were 15,000 doctors who would make guinea pigs of their patients by testing a new proprietary laxative on them, all 15,000 should be deprived of their licenses and put in jail for gross negligence.

"Scientist's Discovery Leads to Perfection of New Product after Years of Research." . . . "A famous laboratory became interested." What scientist? What laboratory? In the absence of names, this claim should be regarded as one more product of a copy-writer's imagination.

"Three-hundred thousand Users as Result of Doctors' Recommendations." How can the manufacturers know this? In the absence of explanation, one would be justified in assuming that this represents the number of free samples sent to doctors, or the number of tins sold to drug stores, or the sum of both.

"Tested and Approved by Bureau of Foods, Sanitation and Health Conducted by . . . . *Good Housekeeping* Magazine." The Bureau also tested and approved Grayban and Vapex. No further consideration need be given this claim.

In another advertisement for Saráka appearing in the November, 1934, issue of *Good Housekeeping* is the statement that Saráka pro-

TESTS BY 15,862* DOCTORS

PROVE SARÁKA IDEAL FOR

CONSTIPATION

Scientist's Discovery Leads to Perfection of New Product after Years of Research

Costs You Only 10¢ to Satisfy Yourself as to Its Merit

Amazing qualities in the sap of a tropical tree led a scientist to believe that he had discovered a natural product that would be valuable in the treatment of constipation. That was in 1911.

A famous laboratory became interested. Years were spent experimenting, testing, refining. At last, using this sap as the basic ingredient, the laboratory perfected a product which, it believed, represented a tremendous advance in the treatment of habitual constipation.

300,000 Users as Result of Doctors Recommendations

Samples were sent to doctors all over the United States. Tests were made by 15,862 physicians. Doctors, having fully satisfied themselves as to its merits, began recommending Saráka to their patients. Solely as a result of doctors recommendations over 300,000 people are using Saráka today.

But we believe there is only one way that *you* can satisfy yourself as to the merits of Saráka and that is by trying it. You be the judge . . . try it . . . test it . . . discuss it with your doctor . . . observe the results. That's why we make this offer.

Our Sample Offer to You

Saráka is now on sale in all drug stores. It comes in two sizes, 75¢ and $1.25. But in order that you may test Saráka before purchasing these larger-size packages, our laboratory has prepared a number of trial-size packages. *If your doctor hasn't given you one* you may buy one at most druggists for 10¢. If you wish, you may obtain one by sending the coupon below.

With each sample there is a folder giving interesting information about habitual constipation and how Saráka may be used to help overcome it. Let Saráka help you.

Copyright 1934 Schering Corporation

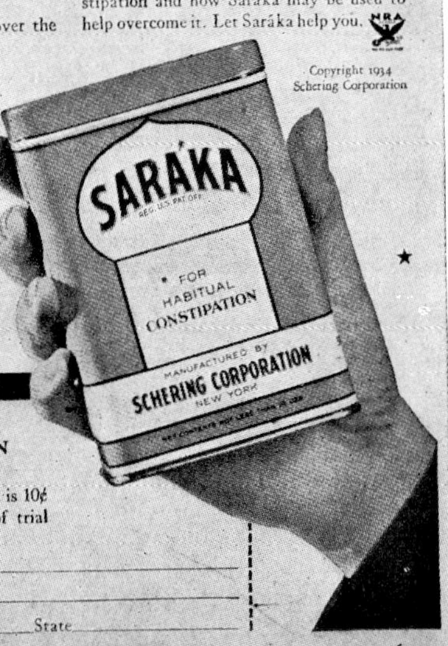

*Up to March 12th, 1934

Tested and Approved Bureau of Foods, Sanitation and Health

SCHERING CORPORATION
Dept. G-8, Bloomfield, N. J.

I'd like to try Saráka. Enclosed is 10¢ to cover postage and mailing of trial package.

Name____________________

Address____________________

City____________ State__________

EVERY product advertised is guaranteed—see page 6

(from *Good Housekeeping,* March, 1934.)

15,862 DOCTORS—300,000 GUINEA PIGS

duces 3 times the bulk of agar-agar. In seeking a key to the possible safety of a laxative which acts by creating bulk in the intestines, it is well to know something about agar-agar. Dr. J. F. Montague says* of agar: ". . . It is absolutely essential to mix the granules or wafers thoroughly with food before taking, as otherwise they are very prone to adhere to each other when moistened and will, thus, roll themselves into a ball which not only does not accomplish the purpose of adding bulk to the bowel residue, but may actually lead in time to the formation of one large mass in the colon. . . .

"In giving my qualified endorsement of agar as a means of increasing the residue of the bowel content, I feel it only fair to point out that unless a sufficient amount of water is taken during the day to allow a thorough mixing with the food and an equally thorough moistening of the agar, there may occur an accumulation of this in the rectum and colon in the form of hardened masses which obstruct the onward passage of the fecal matter and, thus, create a very disturbing situation. . . . It will be found that if too large doses are taken there is a real danger of having the bowel movements so large that they are not only difficult of passage, but may actually damage the delicate lining of the rectum."

Since it is claimed that Saráka expands three times as much as agar, the possible hazards of Saráka may be many times as great. In view of the gross disregard for the consumer's welfare shown by the patent medicine industry, for anyone to accept the assurance of *any* advertiser as to the safety of a medicinal product is little short of insanity.

How the Average Reader Should Analyze the Saráka Advertisement:

"Another scientific discovery where they forget to tell even the scientist's name. Probably the usual bunk. It's new. That means they want to make a guinea pig out of me. No, thanks."

---

* Dr. J. F. Montague, *I Know Just the Thing for That.* John Day Company, N. Y.

32. Analyze The Ads

ADVERTISING can be read with profit if it is carefully analyzed. To start with, analyze the advertisements reproduced on the following pages in the light of what you have read thus far. Imagine that you are considering purchasing the products advertised, and are trying to make up your mind whether or not to buy on the basis of the information given in the advertisements. Pick every statement to pieces. Ask yourself such questions as these: Is it clear, definite, and informing, or does it attempt to mislead me with vague hints or claims of perfection? If definite statements are made, what *evidence* is given that they did not originate only in the mind of the copy-writer? What information do I really need about the product? How much of this information does the advertisement give? If it is a food, medical, or cosmetic product is it advertised as a new development or discovery? In other words, is the advertiser trying to make a guinea pig out of me (assuming his claim of newness is not the usual hokum)?

If it is a new mechanical or electrical product (a new type of oil burner, for instance) what evidence is given that it was thoroughly tested under conditions of use so that you won't have to do the manufacturer's testing for him at *your* expense? (New mechanical products of even the largest companies usually require redesign to correct serious faults after the products are tried out on early customers.) If there is a guarantee, exactly what does it mean? Is the advertisement garnished with SCIENCE? If the scientists are not American scientists with whose names and reputations (apart from advertising "science") you are familiar, discount the claims 100 percent. Even if scientists of reputation are directly quoted, discount the claims at least 90 percent. What is actually said *may* be true, but when the pay check is large enough even distinguished professors may have easy consciences about permitting the suppression of vital information of a negative nature which the consumer should have. And remember that advertisements can appear in newspapers and magazines which maintain Institutes, Bureaus, and "Scrutinizers" and still be 100 percent false.

"A BEAUTY CREAM IRRADIATED WITH

ULTRA-VIOLET RAYS

. . . what marvelous things that would do for a woman!"

said Barbara Gould

—and with a university scientist she developed her new Irradiated Skin Food, *which all night long sheds tiny rays upon your skin, though you can't* see *them or* feel *them!*

EVERY physician in the world knows about the remarkable *re-vitalizing* power which lies in the ultra-violet rays of sunshine.

"If a woman's skin could be treated with *just the right amount* of tiny ultra-violet rays all the year 'round" said Barbara Gould, "what radiantly clear, youthful skin she could have!"

So, in collaboration with a university scientist, she developed a skin food irradiated with just enough ultra-violet rays to *benefit* the skin without tanning it!

First, you cleanse your skin with Barbara Gould s filmy Cleansing Cream. It liquefies the instant it touches the skin and removes the impurities from the pores.

Then—pat the new Irradiated Skin Food over your face and neck, and allow it to remain during the night. *While you sleep,* rays are gently, slowly, safely, shed upon your skin. But so *mild* are these rays, so safe, that they give only the benefits of sunshine, without tanning, without giving you a sunburn. Try this marvelous new Irradiated Skin Food *tonight!*

Barbara Gould

Barbara Gould Irradiated Skin Food—
$2.75 for a Generous Jar—Smaller Size $1.25
Irradiated Face Powder—$1.65
Barbara Gould Cleansing, Finishing, Tissue and Circulation Creams—
$1.10 the Jar—50¢ the Tube

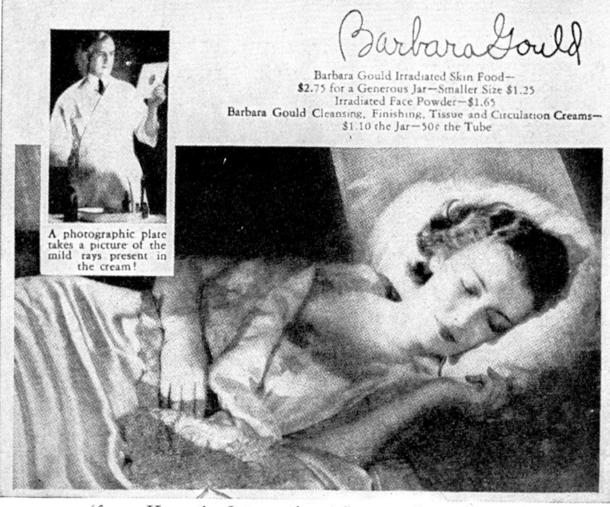

A photographic plate takes a picture of the mild rays present in the cream!

(from Hearst's *International-Cosmopolitan,* November, 1934.)

AN EASY ONE TO ANALYZE

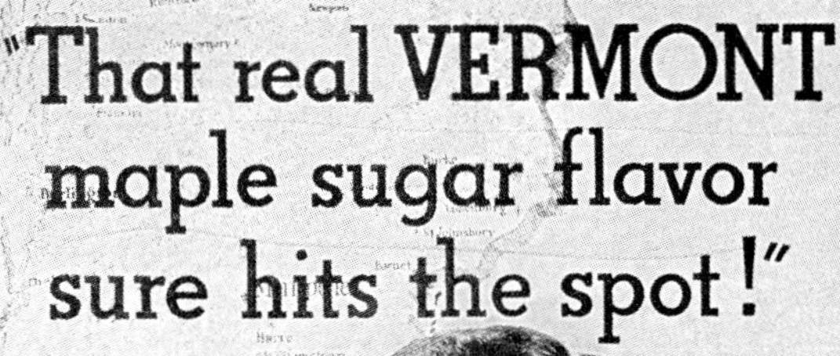

"That real VERMONT
maple sugar flavor
sure hits the spot!"

Straight from Vermont's maple sugar district comes this delicious blend of pure cane and Vermont maple sugars

EVER SINCE the early settling of America—the state of Vermont has been famous for its fine big maple trees—its delicious maple sugar.

Today—in the heart of the maple sugar district—on the shore of Lake Champlain—Vermont Maid Syrup is blended for your table.

Pure sparkling maple sugar is skillfully combined with the choicest cane sugar—to produce this syrup with that good old maple tang you love so well.

How good it tastes—as it trickles over a crisp, hot waffle—mingling its maple sugar flavor with melting butter.

Ask your grocer for Vermont Maid Syrup. It comes in attractive glass jugs—ready for the table. You can buy no finer syrup. Penick & Ford, Ltd., Inc., Burlington, Vt.

★ **Vermont Maid Syrup**

EVERY product advertised is guaranteed—see page 6

(from *Good Housekeeping,* February, 1935.)

VERMONT . . . VERMONT . . . VERMONT

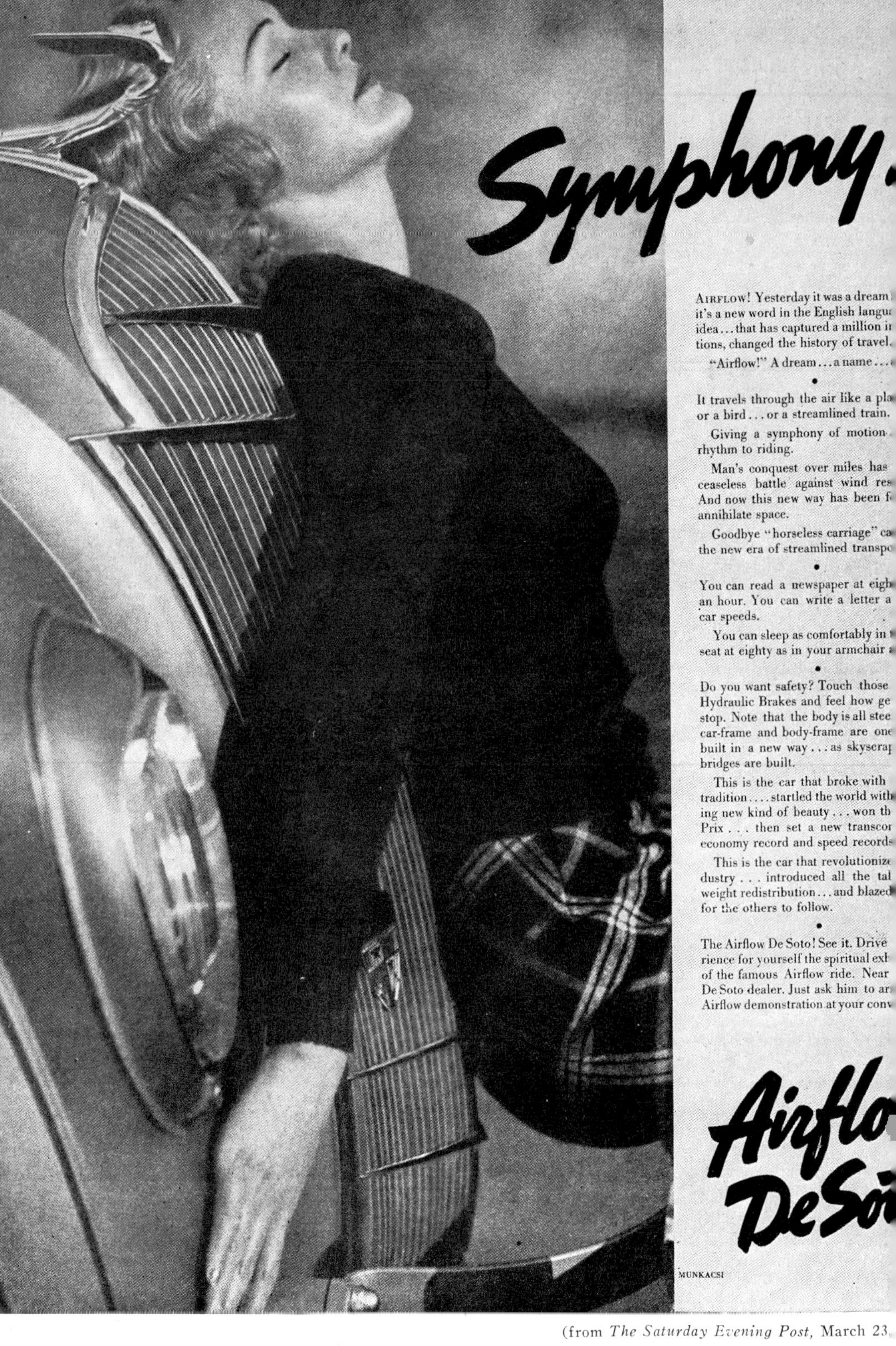

(from *The Saturday Evening Post,* March 23

LITERARY CRITICS MIGHT TRY THIS ONE

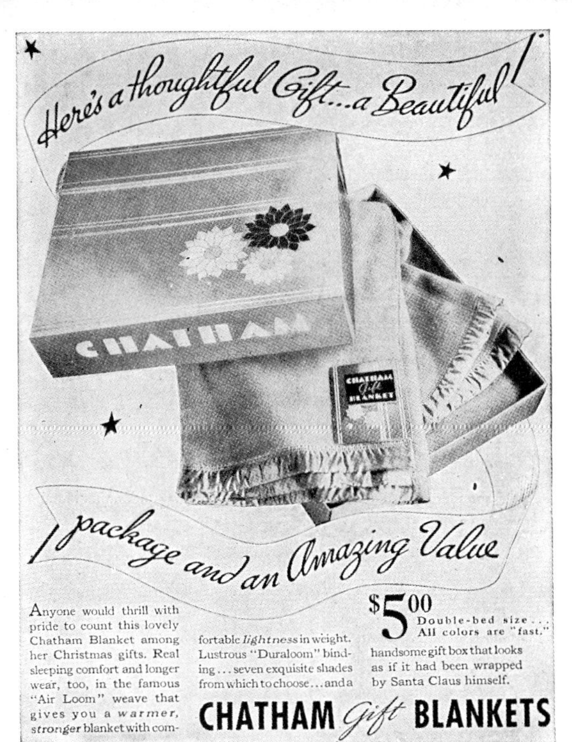

(from *The Ladies Home Journal,* December, 1934.)

LOOK A GIFT HORSE IN THE MOUTH

DON'T TREAT A HEADACHE BLINDLY!

B. C. Contains Several Ingredients—Not Just One—Attacks Headaches and Neuralgia on All Fronts

Your physician will verify these facts on headaches. A headache may be due to *a number* of different causes. You seldom know *which* cause—or which *combination of causes*—is responsible.

Many headache remedies are based on only *one* ingredient. Often that one ingredient does not effectively reach the cause of *your* headache.

Because of these facts, the formula for B. C. was developed—based on a physician's prescription. Several ingredients of proven effectiveness are skilfully blended. Each strikes at one or more types of headache. In combination they strike at virtually *all* types.

None of these ingredients are opiates or narcotics—but they do relieve headaches and similar inorganic aches and pains with amazing rapidity.

When you take B. C. you are attacking a headache on *all* fronts. You get relief far more quickly—usually in three or four minutes.

B. C. is the fastest-selling product of its kind on the market. Millions praise it. Benefit by their experience. Use B. C. at first sign of a headache—simple head cold—or neuralgia.

Discover how quickly this *prescription-type* remedy brings relief. In 10c and 25c packages. Ask your druggist for B. C. today.

TUNE IN Sam Taylor's "Hollywood Highlights" WMCA Mondays and Wednesdays at 6:30. Free pictures of movie stars!

(from *The World Telegram,* January 25, 1934.)

NO, DON'T TREAT A HEADACHE BLINDLY

33. A Few Tests

Goods counterfeiting is successful partly because the consumer can seldom detect a counterfeit. There are, however, a few simple tests for textiles which the consumer can use. When considering the purchase of a woolen garment, you may be able to detach a strand from the unfinished edge of an inside seam. If this strand breaks easily, the fabric itself is probably weak and is likely to wear poorly. Or if the individual hair-like fibers in the strand are short (about an inch or less in length), the fabric is probably woven largely of salvaged and reworked wool, and little wear can be expected.

If you can get a sample of a fabric before you buy, or wish to check a guarantee afterward, you can, with nothing more than a match, test for "all-wool" or "pure-silk." Cotton flares and burns rapidly; wool chars but does not burn, and gives off a characteristic odor. Pure silk or silk with little metallic weighting "melts" into

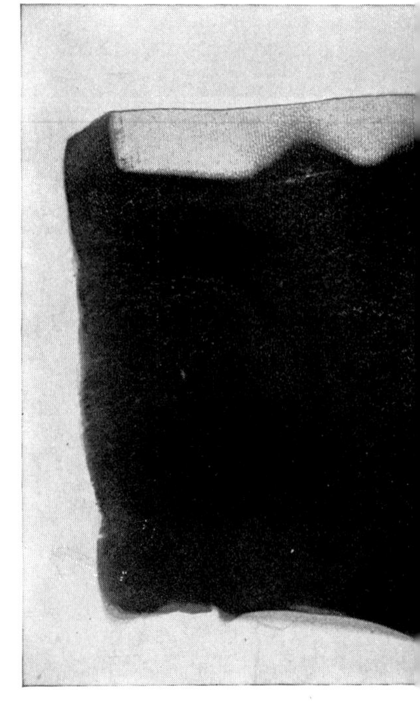

Left—Silk After Burning; Right—Weighted Silk After Burning

Testing Silk

more or less spherical black lumps. Heavily weighted silk simply appears to blacken, the metallic framework retaining the form of the unburned fabric.

As problems at once useful and educational, high school and college physics, chemistry, and home economics classes might well work on simple methods of test for various kinds of consumer goods, from textiles to vacuum cleaners.

34. Make It Yourself

OFTEN a single, inexpensive chemical or a simple combination of chemicals of unquestioned utility becomes a costly counterfeit by the addition of a fancy package and an advertising campaign based on absurd claims. There is no better means of understanding this type of counterfeit (and of saving a few dollars or cents) than by the purchase of the chemicals under their own honest names and the preparation of a few simple products. This is especially worth while for consumer clubs and for classes, and the following examples are primarily for their benefit:

Fly-Spray. An excellent fly spray of the Flit type can be easily made with the two ingredients shown in the photograph, pyrethrum powder and kerosene. The proportions are two ounces of the powder to each quart of kerosene. The pyrethrum powder can be purchased in many drug stores, at between 50 and 75 cents for a half-pound, and the kerosene at gasoline filling stations for about 15 cents per gallon. Simply pour the powder into the kerosene and let it stand. The powder will settle to the bottom of the container. Pour or siphon off the clear liquid, which is then ready for use. Cost, 15 to 22 cents per quart. The price of Flit is about one dollar per quart.

Floor Wax. The ingredients of U. S. government specification floor wax of a far better grade than you are likely to be able to buy are illustrated on page 88. They are gasoline (not leaded gasoline), 9 ounces; turpentine, 9 ounces; carnauba wax, 6 ounces; and ceresin wax, 6 ounces. These amounts will nearly fill an empty coffee tin, which is adequate both for mixing and for storing the wax. Of course, more or less wax can be made by increasing or decreasing the quantities while retaining the same proportions.

Don't work near a flame. All of the melting should be done with boiling water. Place the waxes in the tin, place the tin in boiling water and stir steadily until the waxes are liquefied, renewing the boiling water several times. (The melting takes a half-hour or more.) When the waxes are completely liquefied, pour in the gasoline and turpentine, put the tin in cold water, and stir vigorously until the wax cools and becomes of paste consistency. A softer paste can be made by using a few more ounces of gasoline.

The necessary waxes can be obtained from any chemical supply house. Many supply houses will fill mail orders by parcel post C.O.D. If there is no chemical supply house in your town, a druggist can

The Ingredients Of Fly Spray

give you the name of one. Carnauba wax by the pound should cost about 75 cents, and ceresin wax about 30 cents. The ingredient cost per pound of finished floor wax is about 25 cents. A comparable wax bought at the store costs about a dollar.

THESE INGREDIENTS MAKE FLOOR WAX

The equivalent of some commercial products can be "made" with no mixing or processing. Trisodium phosphate, an excellent cleansing powder available at chemical supply houses for about 8 cents per pound in 25-pound lots, is sold in the grocery store as Oakite at 11 cents for a 14-ounce package. (The car-lot price of trisodium phosphate to a manufacturer is about 2.5 cents per pound.)

Clubs and classes will enjoy "making" talcum powder equal to almost any that can be purchased. The cost will be about 20 cents per pound (Colgate's Cashmere Talcum Powder costs 19 cents for three ounces.) Italian talc, the best available, can be bought from chemical supply houses at about 15 cents per pound. A high grade of essential oil, better than that used in most of the widely advertised brands of talcum powder, such as lavender (one of the least expensive oils, U. S. Pharmacopoeia grade of natural lavender costing 45 cents per ounce), jasmine, or violet, can be purchased for less than one dollar for a one-ounce bottle; and an ounce is enough for about 50 pounds of powder. The oil (about six drops per pound) is first mixed with a small amount of powder, put through a fine sieve if necessary for smoothness, and then added to the bulk of the powder and thoroughly mixed with it.

The making of floor waxes, fly sprays, and other household articles is an excellent activity for boys' and girls' clubs and for domestic science classes in schools. Ingredients for an entire group can be purchased in quantity from chemical supply houses at prices much lower than pound-lot prices. Work of this type would be somewhat better educationally than the distribution of breakfast food samples and the study of "scientific" booklets and posters supplied by breakfast food companies.

MELTING THE WAXES

35. But It Doesn't Work

THE consumer must face the fact that goods counterfeiting is a part of the structure of our economic system, and cannot be ended by wishes, laws, or books like this one. An activity such as that of Consumers' Research cannot wipe out goods counterfeiting; it can only give consumers a measure of personal defense against some counterfeiters. There is one other defense which theoretically is excellent and needs to be described here. It is called "standardization."

Let us take a concrete example. You want to buy an overcoat. What is a good overcoat? First, it should be warm. Second, it should wear well, resisting tearing and fraying. Third, it should be well sewn, with seams that will not rip apart and pockets that will stay on. Fourth, the dyes should be light-fast and water-fast. Fifth, it should have a lining which will wear as long as the coat. There is, of course, the additional factor of style, but that factor you can judge yourself. Of the other five factors, however, you cannot now adequately judge a single one at the time of purchase.

Yet every one of these factors is measurable with an accuracy more than sufficient for your needs. There are instruments for testing the heat-insulating properties of a fabric. There are others that test resistance to breaking both of fabric and of seams and resistance to tear and abrasion. Finally, the fastness of the dye can be measured. It thus becomes possible to establish a technical standard for overcoat quality expressed, not in glowing advertising phrases, but in definite units of measure. A coat that would give three years' wear and provide adequate warmth at a temperature of, say, 20 degrees with a 20-mile wind blowing might be taken as the standard. It would be a complicated but not an over-difficult job to determine approximately what figures for warmth, strength, and dye fastness would meet this standard. These figures would then be included, along with size specifications to assure proper fit in what might be called the "National Standard for Overcoat Quality." Then various overcoat manufacturers would submit samples of their products for test, and all coats that met the standards would be labeled: "This coat meets the requirements of the National Standard for Overcoat Quality." Then you could go into a shop and ask for coats meeting this standard, and buy one knowing that it should provide satisfactory warmth at temperatures over 20 degrees and last at least three years.

But this would be only the first step. Suppose you lived in the mountains and wanted a warmer coat, or your occupation subjected your coat to extraordinary wear, and you wanted a stronger coat. Or suppose you wore flannel underwear and needed a lighter coat? This standard would be of little help to you, and again you would be forced to rely on the word of a salesman who might know no more than you about warmth, quality, and wear.

So we find that a second step would be needed. It is *grading*. Instead of establishing one standard, we would establish, say, five standards for five different grades of wear and warmth. For example,

Grade 1. Standardized in terms of a temperature of *20 degrees below zero,* and *five years'* wear.
Grade 2. Standardized in terms of a temperature of *20 degrees below zero,* and *three years'* wear.
Grade 3. Standardized in terms of a temperature of *20 degrees above zero,* and *five years'* wear.
Grade 4. Standardized in terms of a temperature of *20 degrees above zero,* and *three years'* wear.
Grade 5. Standardized in terms of a temperature of *40 degrees above zero,* and *three years'* wear.

In cold climates, stores would specialize in the first two grades; in warmer areas, in the last three; and every coat would bear a label showing the grade. When you paid your money for a grade 3 coat, you would know what you were getting. There would be no more dependence on advertisers' and salesmen's claims, no more talk about "superb quality, unexcelled wear." If you wished to have your coat cut by a tailor you would still have that privilege.

A beautiful picture, isn't it? It has only one flaw—it wouldn't work. Grades can be established in two ways; by government action, as egg and milk grades were; or by voluntary agreement of the producers and distributors to use grades. The government will not impose standards for manufactured consumer goods customarily sold by advertising so long as manufacturers, publishers, advertisers and their business and banking colleagues control Congress and the State legislatures, and there is no reason to expect the end of such control. If, under extraordinary pressure, following gross and obvious abuses, a standard should be imposed by the government (through the N.R.A., for example) you can be sure that it will not generally be necessary to improve products to bring them up to standard; the standard will be set low enough to cover existing products—at least, the products of large manufacturers. Even then, should considerable business losses to any large producer impend, the standard will be modified, set aside, or simply ignored.

In theory, the method of voluntary agreement by producers and distributors is quite perfect, and established machinery to expedite the functioning of this method already exists. In brief, the method is this. Some organization of consumers, for example, the American Home Economics Association, decides that consumers are sadly in need of standards to aid in the purchase of, let us say, silk. The Home Economics Association writes to the American Standards Association, telling in polite language how crooked the silk industry is, and how it is defrauding consumers, and asking the Standards Association to bring about the establishment of standards for silk.

It is the rule of the Association to proceed with a standardization project only if practically all important groups of producers and distributors concerned approve. Silk manufacturers, dyers, dress manufacturers, retailers, and other business groups, as well as consumer groups, are therefore asked whether they agree that standards should be developed. If they do, with fair unanimity, the Association forms a technical committee on which the producers, the distributors, and the consumers have equal representation. Equal, that is to say, in numbers; but there the equality ends. For the consumers *want* a standard, and it takes unanimous agreement of all the parties, including the producers, to give the consumers what they want. The *producers* want the standardization effort killed (for it would interfere with their defrauding of the consumer) and any one party—meaning themselves—can kill a standard. If, for political reasons, the producers condescend to accept a standard, it is a "compromise" standard, meaning one providing nothing which will greatly help consumers or greatly interfere with producers. And to cap it all, if a standard is developed and approved, there is nothing to make the producers and distributors use it.

As a matter of fact, the American Standards Association actually was requested by the American Home Economics Association to establish standards for silk. A conference to consider the request was called, and the producers refused to have anything to do with it. That was the end of the project. Another project, now under way, contemplates the establishment of standards for domestic refrigerators. Standards may indeed be developed, but all the signs point toward "compromise" standards,—low enough to cover all nationally advertised refrigerators without any important modifications, and which will be of not the slightest aid to the average consumer in deciding whether to buy a "monitor-topped" General Electric or a "Rollator" Norge.

In the field of industrial products used by industry itself, steel rails or electric cable, for example, the methods of the American Standards Association are quite successful, for here the consumer is not the unorganized, technically ignorant, easily exploited individual household buyer, but a closely organized, technically competent, and economically powerful group—the railways and power companies, for example, which can meet the producers on equal (and often superior) terms.

Even more futile than the efforts of the American Standards Association on behalf of consumers are similar efforts on the part of the United States Bureau of Standards, skilled as it is in serving the needs of business and politics.

Standardization does not work for the consumer in a profit economy.

36. There Ought To Be A Law

MANY readers of this book will feel cheated because no simple remedies to end goods counterfeiting are proposed. There are no simple remedies.

We like to look to legislation to cure our economic and social ills. But legislation can be as much a counterfeit as money or goods. Soon after President Roosevelt was inaugurated, he initiated legislation which, the public was led to believe, would end the robbing and poisoning of consumers of foods, drugs, and cosmetics. This legislation was then turned over by the administration to Senator Royal S. Copeland, probably the only man in the entire Congress who was *at that very time openly in the employ of fake medical advertisers.* Needless to say, the Senator has done his duty by his employers, and if a food, drug, and cosmetic law is passed, it will almost certainly be a counterfeit, protecting the big producers, not consumers.

But suppose that a good law for the control of foods, drugs, and cosmetics were passed. Counterfeiting and business profits would still be protected by a number of means now available and regularly used. The law would be hamstrung in business-controlled courts; every imaginable kind of pressure would prevent officials from properly enforcing the law except against small and unimportant offenders (assuming that the officials were willing to jeopardize their jobs by strict enforcement); persuaded by powerful food and drug lobbies that the time had at last come for the Government to practice economy, Congress would neglect to appropriate enough money for adequate enforcement; and finally, if these and other means failed to protect business profits, the teeth of the law would be drawn by Congressional amendments.

It is hopeless to look for legislative remedies. The whole trouble is that goods counterfeiting is not an isolated phenomenon. The robbing and the poisoning of the consumer, the paying of starvation wages to workers, the closing of schools to avoid heavy taxes on business, the destruction of huge quantities of food while children go hungry—these are all related symptoms of progressing and incurable disease in an economic organism built up to safeguard profits for the few who have wealth and power without regard for the welfare of the millions. The remedy must be sought not in legislation, but in a fundamental change in our economic system.*

---

* Not primarily because of goods counterfeiting, however; more because so many are unable to buy even counterfeit goods.

But again we bump up against the counterfeiters, who now use heavy doses of sodium sulphite on a rapidly decaying economy, and make it look worth saving; who offer us such counterfeit remedies

© Acme

SENATOR COPELAND BROADCASTING FOR ENO SALTS
(while the Copeland bill grows weaker and weaker)

as the "New Deal" and the N.R.A., "helping" the consumer by raising prices and increasing the profits of corporations; who may finally offer the supreme counterfeit—fascism.

In the opinion of the author, goods counterfeiting cannot be ended so long as it pays; that is, so long as industry is privately owned * and profits are the motivating force behind production; and to suggest any easy remedy would be to offer only one more counterfeit to consumers.

* The reader may ask the pertinent question as to how completely goods counterfeiting has been eliminated along with private industry in Soviet Russia. It is to be hoped that thoroughgoing studies of consumer relations in that country will help to clarify the problem.

Index